M000198500

Manopubbaṅgamā dhammā,
manoseṭṭhā manomayā;
Manasā ce paduṭṭhena,
bhāsati vā karoti vā;
Tato naṃ dukkhamanveti,
cakkaṃva vahato padaṃ.

Manopubbaṅgamā dhammā,
manoseṭṭhā manomayā;
Manasā ce pasannena,
bhāsati vā karoti vā;
Tato naṃ sukhamanveti
chāyāva anapāyinī.

Mind precedes everything; mind matters most.
Whatever one experiences throughout life
is nothing but the product of one's own mind.
If one speaks or acts with an impure mind,
suffering will follow,
even as the wheel follows the hoof of the ox.

… If one speaks or acts with a pure mind,
happiness follows like an inseparable shadow.

—*Dhammapada* 1.1-2

Dedication

This anthology of stories, discourses, and poems about death, and preparing for death through Vipassana meditation, is dedicated to Mr. S.N. Goenka. He willingly embraced his teacher Sayagyi U Ba Khin's mission to introduce Vipassana meditation throughout the world, and with open hands joyfully shared the teaching of the Buddha.

This book is also dedicated to those who faced their own deaths or the deaths of loved ones, and whose stories inspire us to take up and diligently practice the Buddha's teaching.

Table of Contents

Appendix

Preface

While we have tried to keep this book as accessible as possible, at times various Pāli and Hindi words are used in the text. These terms are defined when they are first presented and included in the glossary at the end of this book. A few of the important terms are also explained below.

Pāli is an ancient Indian language in which the texts recording the teaching of the Buddha are preserved. Historical, linguistic, and archaeological evidence indicates that Pāli was spoken in northern India at or near the time of the Buddha. The references for the Pāli verses included in this book are from the Vipassana Research Institute's edition of the Pāli Tipiṭaka.

Dhamma (Sanskrit, Dharma) means phenomenon; object of mind; nature; natural law; law of liberation, i.e., teaching of an enlightened person.

Dohas (poetic rhymed couplets) date back to the beginnings of Indian literature. The *dohas* included in this book were composed and are chanted by S.N. Goenka in Hindi. They are often heard during the morning break at Vipassana meditation centers in India.

S.N. Goenka
1924–2013

About S.N. Goenka

Satya Narayan Goenka (affectionately called "Goenkaji" by his students) was a teacher of Vipassana meditation in the tradition of Sayagyi U Ba Khin of Myanmar.

Although Indian by descent, Goenkaji was born and raised in Myanmar. While living there he had the good fortune to come into contact with U Ba Khin, and to learn the technique of Vipassana from him. After receiving training from his teacher for 14 years, Goenkaji settled in India and began teaching Vipassana in 1969. In a country still sharply divided by differences of caste and religion, the courses offered by Goenkaji attracted thousands of people from every part of society. In addition, many people from countries around the world came to join courses in Vipassana meditation.

Goenkaji taught tens of thousands of people in more than 300 courses in India and in other countries, East and West. In 1982 he began to appoint assistant teachers to help him to meet the growing demand for courses. Meditation centers were established under his guidance in India, Canada, the United States, Australia, New Zealand, France, the United Kingdom, Japan, Sri Lanka, Thailand, Myanmar, Nepal and other countries.

The technique taught by S.N. Goenka represents a tradition that is traced back to the Buddha. The Buddha never taught a sectarian religion; he taught Dhamma—the way to liberation—which is universal. In the same tradition, Goenkaji's approach is totally non-sectarian. For this reason, his teaching has had a profound appeal to people of all backgrounds, of every religion and no religion, and from every part of the world.

In his lifetime, Goenkaji was the recipient of many honors but insisted that they were all really for the Dhamma.

S.N. Goenka peacefully breathed his last on Sunday evening September 29, 2013, at his home in Mumbai, India. He was in his 90th year and had served half his life as a teacher of Vipassana meditation. His legacy will continue as long as people around the world seek to learn the teaching of liberation.

The Passing of the Day

Following is an account of how Shri Satya Narayan Goenka faced his last moments, on Sunday, September 29, 2013.

Sometimes the end of life comes as peacefully as the passing of the day.

In the last months of his long life, Goenkaji was confined to a wheelchair and faced increasing pain, yet he strove to carry on with his daily routine. Often he had recalled how the Buddha served until his last moments. It was clear that Goenkaji intended to follow that great example. He continued to meet with visitors and to take a close interest in the Dhamma work.

On his last day, at breakfast time Goenkaji asked his son Shriprakash how work was proceeding at the Global Vipassana Pagoda. Shriprakash replied that he would be visiting the Global Pagoda that day and would make a full report on his return.

During the day, Goenkaji worked on a selection of 500 of his *dohas* (couplets) for possible future publication. As always, this was a labor of love for him.

At lunch, Goenkaji said, "I am relieved of the doctors." Mataji attached no special significance to these words; she thought he was referring to a particular doctor who had recently visited him. However, it was obvious that Goenkaji wanted to spend the day quietly, undisturbed.

After teatime, Goenkaji reviewed major stories in the newspapers, as he was accustomed to do every day. He then meditated in a chair in his room. He came to the table for the evening meal but kept silent during it and returned directly to his room afterwards.

He remained seated there for some time and then asked to be helped to bed. As soon as he was lying down, he started breathing faster. Noticing this when she entered the room, Mataji asked Shriprakash to come. Goenkaji opened his eyes and recognized his son but spoke no word. Shriprakash called the family doctor, and then a doctor who lived in the same building and was able to come at once. But events moved swiftly to their end. The breath came in, the breath went out and then ceased. The heart had stopped beating. There was no sign of pain or stress on Goenkaji's face, and the atmosphere in the room was serene and peaceful. The time was 10:40 p.m.—the end of the day and a fitting close to a long life of Dhamma.

About This Book

For many years my husband and I were editors of the *Vipassana Newsletter*. This afforded us a unique opportunity to hear and see many inspiring stories about meditators who had died bravely and peacefully, filled with the wisdom of their meditation practice. We have read accounts of the deaths of parents, partners, children and friends. Often, as they witnessed their beloved die with contentment and equanimity, those present were filled with an unexpected happiness on an occasion of irreplaceable loss.

The Buddha said, “Two things only do I teach: misery and the way out of misery.” This collection of writings—Goenkaji’s explanations of the teaching of the Buddha, the Buddha’s scriptural verses, poetical stories of monks and nuns from the time of the Buddha, accounts from fellow meditators—is born of the acceptance of the truth of suffering. It contains inspiring examples of people gaining strength and a taste of freedom through their practice, and demonstrates convincingly the efficacy of the Path, the way out of misery.

I have gathered these stories not only to help sustain and strengthen established Vipassana meditators in their quest, but also to encourage others searching for peace and understanding to take up the practice of getting to “know thyself” truly, on an experiential level—to develop their own wisdom.

May you experience the fruits of the Path taught by the Buddha: freedom from the suffering and sorrow that we face throughout our lives.

—Virginia Hamilton

January 2014

About Vipassana Meditation

Vipassana, which means to see things as they really are, is one of India's most ancient techniques of meditation. It was rediscovered by Gotama Buddha more than 2,500 years ago, who taught it as a universal remedy for universal ills—an "art of living."

This nonsectarian technique aims for the total eradication of mental impurities and the resultant highest happiness of full liberation. Its purpose is not the mere curing of disease, but the essential healing of human suffering.

Vipassana is a method of self-transformation through self-observation. It focuses on the deep interconnection between mind and body. This mind-and-body connection can be experienced directly by disciplined attention to the physical sensations that form the life of the body, and that continuously condition the life of the mind. It is this observation-based, self-exploratory journey to the common root of mind and body that dissolves mental impurity, resulting in a balanced mind full of love and compassion.

The scientific laws that underlie one's thoughts, feelings, judgments and sensations become evident. How one grows or regresses, how one produces suffering or frees oneself from suffering, is understood through direct experience. Life becomes characterized by increased self-control, awareness, non-delusion, and peace.

—www.dhamma.org

My Mother's Death in Dhamma

In 1985 a student asked Goenkaji whether it is possible to feel sensations at the time of death. In reply, he related the following story about his adoptive mother's death (previously published in the April 1992 issue of the Vipassana Newsletter*).*

I am one of six sons. I was adopted at a young age by my uncle and aunt, Mr. Dwarkadas and Mrs. Ramidevi Goenka, who at the time had six daughters but no son.

My adoptive mother was a devoted student of my teacher Sayagyi U Ba Khin. She made great progress in her years of practicing Vipassana under Sayagyi's guidance, and Sayagyi was quite fond of her. As far as is known, she was the only student of Sayagyi to die in his presence.

In 1967, when my mother was about 70 years old, she was diagnosed with an advanced stage of liver cancer. We in the family did not know how long she had suffered because she never complained. It was only a week before her death that she casually spoke about some pain in the area of her liver. When her daughter-in-law (my wife, Mrs. Goenka) asked her to describe the pain, she replied, "Well, the pain is similar to what a mother suffers when she gives birth—except this has no break."

By then she had been meditating very seriously for seven years. She went to the meditation center every time there was a course, whether for 10 days, one month, or any other period. Her bag was always packed. She also did self-courses at home. Although she came from a devout Hindu background, she was no longer interested in rites and rituals; she had left them behind.

From the time she was diagnosed with cancer until she died seven days later, she would not allow anyone to talk to her about her disease. She gave strict orders that only Vipassana meditators were to come into her room, and then only to meditate. They could meditate for a half hour, an hour or many hours, and then were to leave quietly.

In our Hindu community it was customary for the friends of a dying person to come to the house to pay respects. My mother was very popular and she had many people wishing to visit her in her final illness. For those who were not meditators, she gave instructions that they were welcome to visit but not come into her room. They could sit quietly outside her door.

My mother was not interested in receiving treatment, but as her son it was my duty to arrange it for her. Every day our family doctor and a specialist visited her. When they questioned her about her pain she said, "Yes, there is pain. So what? *Anissa, anissa* (the Burmese pronunciation of the *Pāḷi* word *anicca*—impermanence)." She attached no importance to it.

One morning the specialist was concerned that the pain of the cancer might be interfering with her sleep. When he asked, "Did you sleep soundly last night?" she answered, "No, I had no sleep." He wrote a prescription for some sleeping pills that she took that night. The next day the doctor came and asked if she had slept, and she replied, "No." Again on the third day he asked, and again she responded, "No."

Even though she did not complain, the doctor was worried that she was not sleeping because she was suffering so much. Not knowing, because of drug shortages, which particular medicine would be available, he wrote prescriptions for three different strong sleeping pills intending that only one pill be purchased. However, all three were available and bought, and by mistake she was given a triple dose. Once more the next morning she reported that, although her eyelids had become heavy, she had not slept all night.

It then occurred to me that the doctor did not understand. To a Vipassana meditator sleep is unimportant, especially on one's deathbed. Despite sedation, my mother's strong determination had kept her alert. She had been practicing Vipassana every moment. I explained to the doctor that sleeping pills would not help, but he couldn't comprehend. He said, "I have given her this strong medicine and even it does not help her sleep. That must mean that she is in great pain." "It's not the pain," I replied. "It is Vipassana that is keeping her awake, aware of her sensations."

As we came out of her room he remarked, "There is something special about your mother. A woman of the same age in a neighboring house also has liver cancer. She is in great misery and cries out in pain. We feel so sorry to see her in this wretched condition, but cannot console her. And here is your mother who, when we come, just smiles."

The night she died, some family members were meditating with her. About 11 pm she said to us, "It's late. All of you go to sleep now." About midnight the nurse who was on duty noticed that there was no pulse in her wrists. She became worried and, thinking death was near, asked, "May I awaken your children?" "No, no," my mother answered. "My time has not yet come. When it does, I will tell you." At 3 am she told the nurse, "Now is the time. Awaken all the family members. I have to go now."

And so we were all awakened. We came and discovered there was no pulse in many parts of her body. We telephoned Sayagyi and the family doctor, who both came quickly. When the doctor arrived, he said she had only a few minutes left.

Sayagyi arrived shortly thereafter. My mother was lying on her back. There was no pulse in her wrists, as in death, but as soon as she saw her teacher she found the strength to raise her hands and fold them together, paying respect to him.

About five minutes before she died she looked at me and said, "I want to sit." I turned to the doctor who advised, "No, in a few minutes she is going to die; let her die peacefully. If you move her, her death will be painful. She is already suffering; leave her." She heard what he said but again told me, "No, let me sit." I thought, "This is her last wish. She doesn't care about the pain, so what the doctor says is unimportant. I must help her sit."

I placed some pillows at her back. With a jerk she sat erect in a meditation position with folded legs and looked at all of us. I asked her, "Do you feel sensations? Do you feel *anissa*?" She raised her hand and touched the top of her head. "Yes, yes, *anissa*." She smiled … and in half a minute she died. In life her face was always aglow. In death, too, there was a radiant glow on her face.

—S.N. Goenka

Soon after his mother's death Goenkaji left Burma to bring the teaching of the Buddha back to India, the land of Buddha's birth. From India, with the help of thousands of Goenkaji's students, it has spread around the world.

Yogā ve jāyatī bhūri,
ayogā bhūrisaṅkhayo.
Etaṃ dvedhāpathaṃ ñatvā,
bhavāya vibhavāya ca;
Tathāttānaṃ niveseyya,
yathā bhūri pavaḍḍhati.

Truly, from meditation wisdom arises;
Without meditation wisdom vanishes.
Knowing this branching path leading to gain or loss,
One should conduct oneself so that wisdom may increase.

—*Dhammapada* 20.282

The Buddha's Wisdom

The Buddha taught Four Noble Truths, applicable to everyone. The First Noble Truth states that inherent in all things are the seeds of dissatisfaction that inevitably lead to suffering, both mental and physical.

This is so, the Buddha realized, because everything in the universe is changing, in a state of constant flux, impermanent and insubstantial. Nothing remains the same even for a moment.

On some personal level we, too, recognize this: a sense that everything is not right, that something is missing, or might be impossible to keep if acquired. Circumstances change; what we previously wanted no longer matters. Control is erratic, if not illusory. Fleeting pleasures give no lasting satisfaction; genuine fulfillment seems remote, elusive and ephemeral—beyond our grasp.

This insecurity impels us to search for something constant, dependable and secure—something pleasant that will guarantee permanent happiness. However, since everything is in perpetual flux, the quest is fundamentally futile. This fact of incessant craving for satisfaction is the Second Noble Truth.

Through his supreme efforts, the Buddha realized the Third Noble Truth: there can be an end to the suffering we experience in life.

The Fourth Noble Truth is the Eightfold Noble Path, the way that leads to real peace and real liberation. This Path has three divisions: *sīla* (morality), *samādhi* (concentration, or mastery over the mind), and *paññā* (wisdom, or purification of mind).

Morality is a training to refrain from actions—mental, verbal and physical—that might harm others or ourselves. Making effort to live a wholesome life is a necessary base for learning to control the mind. The second division of the Path is development of concentration, a deeper training to calm the mind and train it to remain one-pointed. The third division, the acquisition of wisdom, is achieved through Vipassana meditation, the technique the Buddha discovered to completely eradicate the conditioning and habit patterns that reinforce our unhappiness and dissatisfaction.

The Buddha said that purification of mind is a long path, one that can take many lifetimes to complete. He taught that we have lived through an incalculable number of lives, cycles upon cycles of life and death—some full of bliss, some tormented, all laced with good and bad, pleasant and unpleasant, all lived in reactive blindness to the reality within.

If we are fortunate enough to hear about Vipassana, if we are ready to learn, to make changes in our lives, we might take the practice to heart and begin to dismantle these patterns of reaction conditioned by ignorance. We notice that we seem happier and more stable, less reactive and more tolerant of others. We want to learn more. We begin to share the Dhamma with others. But common questions persist: How will I be at death? Will I be serene? Will I be strong enough to face death peacefully?

Death, the inevitable ending of life, is feared by nearly all. It is often mired in pain and suffering, of both body and mind. Yet the Buddha taught that death is a pivotal moment on the path to freedom from suffering.

At the moment of death a very strong *saṅkhāra* (mental conditioning) will arise in the conscious mind. This *saṅkhāra* generates the necessary impetus for new consciousness to arise in the next life, a consciousness bearing the qualities of this *saṅkhāra*. If the *saṅkhāra* is characterized by unhappiness or negativity, the new consciousness will arise in similar negativity and unhappiness. If, on the other hand, it is replete with virtue and contentment, then this rebirth is likely to be wholesome and happy.[1]

Developing a balanced moment-to-moment awareness of the impermanence of physical sensations in our daily lives, even in the most difficult situations, also creates very deep *saṅkhāras*—positive ones. If the *saṅkhāra* of awareness with the understanding of *anicca* (the constantly changing nature of all

---

[1] Whether we believe in rebirth or not, practicing Vipassana meditation makes our lives easier to live no matter what the situation. We learn how to establish a balanced mind that becomes a strong habit pattern that will help us through all of life's challenges, even death.

things) is strengthened and developed, then this *saṅkhāra* will arise at death to give a positive push into the next life. The mental forces at the instant of death will carry us, as Goenkaji says, "magnetically," into a next life in which Vipassana can continue to be practiced.

Walking on the Eightfold Noble Path is an art of living. Living a life in Dhamma—a life of virtue, awareness, and equanimity—not only enhances our daily existence, it also prepares us for the moment of death and for the next life. A calm awareness of *anicca* at death is a telling measure of progress in mastering the art of living, of progress on the path of peace, the path to *nibbāna*.

Āo logoṅ jagata ke,
caleṅ Dharama ke pantha.
Isa patha calate satpuruṣha,
isa patha calate santa.

Dharma pantha hī śhānti patha.
Dharma pantha sukha pantha.
Jisane pāyā Dharma patha,
maṅgala milā ananta.

Āo mānava-mānavī,
caleṅ Dharama ke pantha.
Kadama-kadama calate hue,
kareṅ dukhoṅ kā anta.

Come, people of the world!
Let us walk the path of Dhamma.
On this path walk holy ones;
on this path walk saints.

The path of Dhamma is the path of peace;
the path of Dhamma is the path of happiness.
Whoever attains the path of Dhamma
gains endless happiness.

Come, men and women!
Let us walk the path of Dhamma.
Walking step by step,
let us make an end of suffering.

—Hindi *dohas* from *Come People of the World*, S.N. Goenka

Yathāpi vātā ākāse vāyanti vividhā puthū;
Puratthimā pacchimā cāpi, uttarā atha dakkhiṇā.
Sarajā arajā capi, sītā uṇhā ca ekadā;
Adhimattā parittā ca, puthū vāyanti mālutā.
Tathevimasmiṃ kāyasmiṃ samuppajjanti vedanā;
Sukhadukkhasamuppatti, adukkhamasukhā ca yā.
Yato ca bhikkhu ātāpi, sampajaññaṃ na riñcati;
Tato so vedanā sabbā, parijānāti paṇḍito.
So vedanā pariññāya diṭṭhe dhamme anāsavo;
Kāyassa bhedā dhammaṭṭho, saṅkhyaṃ nopeti vedagū.

Through the sky blow many different winds,
from east and west, from north and south,
dust-laden and dustless, cold as well as hot,
fierce gales and gentle breezes—many winds blow.
In the same way, in this body, sensations arise,
pleasant, unpleasant, and neutral.
When a meditator, practicing ardently,
does not neglect the faculty of thorough understanding,
then such a wise person fully comprehends all sensations,
and having fully comprehended them,
within this very life becomes freed from all impurities.
At life's end, such a person, being established
in Dhamma and understanding sensations perfectly,
attains the indescribable stage.

—*Paṭhama-ākāsa Sutta, Saṃyutta Nikāya* 1.260

Ahaṅkāra hī janma kā,
jarā mṛityū kā mūla.
Ahaṅkāra mite binā,
miṭe na bhāva-bhaya śhūla.

Self-centeredness is the root
of birth, decay and death.
Unless ego is removed,
the torment and fear of becoming will not end.

—Hindi *doha,* S.N. Goenka

Graham Gambie
1937–1986

As It Was / As It Is

On June 27, 1986, assistant teacher of Vipassana Graham Gambie died after a short illness.

Graham was among the earliest Western students of S.N. Goenka. After his first Vipassana course at Bodhgaya in 1971, Graham remained in India. From the time Dhamma Giri was purchased in November 1974, he lived, served and meditated there for the next five years. He was one of the first assistant teachers appointed by Goenkaji and, after returning to Australia in 1979, he worked tirelessly to help develop Dhamma Bhūmi, the first Vipassana center "down under."

Graham was known to meditators around the world, many of whom he inspired with his Dhamma insight and enthusiasm. What follows is a brief memoir by Graham about his growth in Dhamma.

The thought arises that nearly twelve years have now gone past since my first tremulous arrival in India. Twelve years. Difficult to understand how it all happened or even what actually happened—but one thing is certain, and that is that it did happen. Twelve years.

Who was that person who arrived, driven out of his sanity by all the horrors of Western life and by his own loveless existence as well, with so many disappointments, with so many failed romances, with such a high opinion of himself, and with such a monstrous collection of memories and fears? What happened to that ape-like ancestor? The question often arises. It does not seem possible that he disappeared. That would be too much to hope for. It seems more likely that he never existed at all beyond the bundle of miseries and false hopes. What actually disappeared were the sufferings of yesterday, and what remains are the sufferings of today: the decay into middle age, the inability to adjust to reality, the shoddy burden of failed ambitions, the passions, the talkativeness.

But over the years has it become any easier to accept the anonymous nature of these miseries—to see that the present person is as unreal as his ludicrous predecessor? Oh no. Who gives in willingly to his own ego death? Who gives up the ghost smilingly, without a struggle? Perhaps that is why there is so little love in the world. All we know are those two phantoms, "You" and "I," and not the dissolution of both, which is love.

There is no claim that in twelve years love and joy have taken full command of this mind so infested, as it is, with negativities. But certainly, a lot of the tension has unwound itself, much of the heat of hate has died down, and much of the fear hidden within has disappeared.

Having the power to produce the problem surely confers the right to apply the remedy also. And the only cure for agitations of one kind or another is silence. Looking back, it seems the real journey was not from one country to another, but from agitation to silence; from doing everything and achieving nothing, to doing nothing and letting everything occur. The simpler it is, the more difficult it is to understand. Only a silent mind can see things as they are, and this is the first and last step, the one and only thing to do: the letting be of being.

So many years spent just sitting as silently as possible, experiencing the terrifying collection of sensations, dreams, grasping, and fears that somehow have given rise to the idea of "Me." Those who have never tried might imagine meditation to produce all kinds of ecstasies, spiritual visions, illuminations, and the kinds of things that books are full of. But the real peace is the relief from the terrifying banalities of everyday life, the petty likes and dislikes, the interminable conversations of the mind, the wished for, the lost, the abandoned.

And behind all that … is there anything beyond? Yes: a simple life getting simpler—an ordinary man finding real peace and happiness where he never looked before: in the ordinary things of life. Actually, there are no "ordinary" things of life. Coming to your senses out of your dreams, you find the ordinary is quite miraculous and the miraculous quite ordinary. It is only then that you realize, as one poet put it, that you are alive in search of life.

There is no magic or miracle beyond plain awareness. What can be more magical than a crystal-clear mind—motionless, silent? What can be more miraculous than to be beyond both the search for pleasure and the avoidance of fear? Many think that magic shows are given only on stage or by some bearded guru, without understanding that they themselves are the magic, the magician, the theatre, the audience, and, for that matter, the world too.

Who, living, has escaped the miseries and pleasures of this beastly/blissful world? Why seek security in a world where everything passes, where every final payment is a handful of dust? Why bother to try? What one cannot change, that one must accept. The choice is to accept it with good or bad grace. How your life would change if you could smile at everything!

Meditation then, like love, is not something that can be twisted to suit the ugly dictatorship of the "I." It has practical by-products, but again like love, its end result is dissolution of the ego and its prison, the world. It is its own end, as love is its own reward. Achievements, success, prestige, and saving the world are all in the domain of the "Me" that wants so much and is capable of so little.

A superficial view of life can see only the miseries that produce pessimism, or pleasures that produce a feeling of optimism. In retrospect, the miseries of this mind seem the most valuable, since it was due to that unbearable pain that the search for a cure began. The pleasures too were helpful: through their brevity and unsatisfactory nature the desire arose to take the medicine, bitter as it is. Beyond hope and fear—the Truth. And slowly, ever so slowly, came the understanding that the disease is only in the mind.

To whom should one attribute all that has happened? Whom can we praise or blame for the inevitable? The law of Truth is a homeless orphan who has the disturbing habit of turning up anywhere, any time, completely uninvited, clothed in the strength of meekness, deafening in silence, invincible and empty-handed. This child is you and me.

And now what is to be done? Where to go from here? Where is forward, where back? What to do with all these possibilities, and with tomorrow? When we can obviously take it no more, shall we go on taking it? When will enough be enough? When will we stop to listen to the poet singing the last song:

In the rising of the light
wake with those who awake,
Or go on in the dream
reaching the other shore
Of the sea which has no other shore.

—Verse by Pablo Neruda, *The Watersong Ends*

Graham's Death

This account by Graham Gambie's widow, Anne Doneman, reveals the peace of mind experienced by a meditator who has reaped the benefits of Dhamma. It was excerpted from a longer piece originally published in Realizing Change—Vipassana Meditation in Action, *Vipassana Research Institute, July 2003, p. 168.*

We returned home to Australia in February and in May conducted a 10-day course. Graham appeared to be in a state of near-total collapse at the beginning of the course. In the meditation hall, he was barely conscious on the dais and when he gave instructions he could not construct a sentence correctly. At night his breathing was barely audible. Our concern grew, and so we telephoned a neurologist in Sydney and made an appointment for the day the course ended, intending to fly to New Zealand on the following day.

Fortunately, by Day 10 Graham was fully alert and apparently totally recovered. After the course we traveled to Sydney and met the neurologist, who initially dismissed the lapse as probable short-term memory loss from which white-collar workers sometimes suffer. However, he ordered a CT brain scan, and while waiting for the results Graham and I enjoyed a special lunch. We returned to the neurologist who, without saying a word, took the films from their folder and placed them on a display panel. He pointed out a tumor that filled what seemed to be 50 percent of the brain's left hemisphere. On top of the tumor was a very large cyst.

I was numb and uncomprehending. Yes, we would cancel our air tickets to New Zealand. Yes, we could get Graham directly into hospital that afternoon. The numbness turned to tears as I phoned to arrange accommodation with dear friends in Sydney. I wasn't making sense explaining to them what was happening, so Graham took the telephone and made the arrangements himself. He was calm and collected.

While getting Graham into hospital and making sure he was comfortable, I somehow managed to be outwardly cheerful. But as soon as I left his company I was in tears again. That night, as I meditated, a deep sense of peace arose that was to stay with me throughout Graham's ordeal. It was not the peace that comes from rationalization or intellectualization; it was just something that "kicked in."

Within two days Graham was under the scalpel. The surgeons were not able to remove the entire tumor and, consequently, the prognosis was not good. The neurosurgeon told us that, due to the nature of the tumor, an astrocytoma, he had a maximum of five years to live—and by the end, mentally, he would be a vegetable.

Such news was devastating, yet he took it in his stride. I once heard him say to visitors, "How can I be attached to this body and mind when they are constantly changing? There is nothing to hold onto." Fellow journalists, workmates, police contacts, and those whom he knew through meditation came to visit him. One colleague remarked, "I came expecting to see a body on the bed and to console him. Instead I ended up telling him all about my problems and forgot about his."

The days passed—and I am grateful to have spent every one of them at his side. He was discharged from hospital but within 10 days was back in again. He was having difficulty with his legs, which had become so tender that he could barely walk.

On the morning of June 27, six weeks after the tumor had been diagnosed, I arrived at the hospital. All I could think of was that I really wanted to be close to him that day—there would be no popping out to run errands. We had a lovely time together, and that night while saying goodbye I felt I couldn't get close enough to him. I hopped up on the side of the bed and began to put on lipstick. He asked, "Why?" I said I wanted to look nice for him. He then went on to say the sweetest things about what a wonderful wife I was and how he felt. I was happy and he was happy. We said goodbye.

After dinner that night I was enjoying the last sip of a hot chocolate. I took a breath and at that moment experienced a deep sense of absolute peace and tranquility. The phone rang, a junior nurse calling—could I come quickly? Graham was having a heart attack (later found to have been caused by a blood clot).

But it was clear that there was really no need to hurry. He was gone.

It was Friday, late. As I traveled to the hospital, neon lights were shining and people were out strolling, window shopping, eating. Feelings of fear and vulnerability arose. Such a casual picture of life could not be trusted. What seemed so real, so permanent, was an illusion. We were all walking on very thin ice, blind to the fact that we could fall through at any moment.

I arrived at the hospital and went upstairs to the room where we had exchanged words only hours before. It was deserted, but I was immediately struck by the vibrancy of the atmosphere. It was entirely clear that no one was there. Though Graham's body lay on the bed, it looked like a cast-off coat that could no longer serve its owner. This was all that remained of the person with whom I had just spent four very special years of my life.

What a wonderful life he had lived. I received letters from people who knew him in the past, each one recounting something that Graham had done to help them. I heard how, when he was traveling in India, he would give his last rupee to someone who needed it, how he used to feed street children with money he received from a small investment he had. When I realized how much he had loved and helped others during the time we had together, it became evident that the wonderful good deeds he had performed had all gone with him.

There were no more tears. How could there be tears? The relationship had come full circle. There was nothing left unsaid or unresolved. Yes, it had been the hardest thing I had ever done, but the fruits were so great and so numerous. I was truly fortunate to have briefly shared my life with such a human being.

At the funeral the pews were full and people lined the walls. They came from all persuasions, from all walks of life, each with his or her own personal reason for being there. It was strange to return home to see his clothes just as he had left them, and to know that there was no one to claim ownership.

—Anne Doneman

Phuṭṭhassa lokadhammehi,
cittaṃ yassa na kampati,
asokaṃ virajaṃ khemaṃ;
etaṃ maṅgalamuttamaṃ.

When faced with life's vicissitudes,
one's mind is unshaken,
free from sorrow, impurity or fear.
This is the highest welfare.

—*Maṇgala Sutta, Sutta Nipāta* 2.271

What Happens at Death

This essay by Goenkaji originally appeared in the Sayagyi U Ba Khin Journal, *Vipassana Research Institute, December 1991, and later in the* Vipassana Newsletter, *April 1992.*

To understand what happens at death, let us first understand what death is. Death is like a bend in a continuous river of becoming. It might appear that death is the *end* of a process of becoming—and certainly it may be so in the case of an *arahant* (a fully liberated being) or a *buddha*—but for an ordinary person this flow of becoming continues even after death. Death puts an end to the activities of one life and the very next instant starts the play of a new life. On one side is the last moment of this life and on the other side is the first moment of the next life. It is as though the sun rises as soon as it sets, with no interval of darkness between. It is as if the moment of death is the close of one chapter in the book of becoming, and another chapter of life opens the very next moment.

Although no simile can exactly convey the process, one might say that this flow of becoming is like a train running on a track. It reaches the station of death and, after slightly decreasing speed for a moment, carries on again with the same speed as before. It does not stop at the station even for an instant. For one who is not an *arahant*, the station of death is not a terminus but a junction from where 31 different tracks diverge. The train, as soon as it arrives at the station, shifts onto one or another of these tracks and continues. This speeding train of becoming, running on the electricity of the kammic reactions of the past, keeps on traveling from one station to the next, on one track or the other—a continuous journey that goes on without ceasing.

This switching of tracks happens automatically. As the melting of ice into water and the cooling of water to form ice happen according to laws of nature, so also the transition from life to life is controlled by set laws of nature. According to these laws, the train not only changes tracks by itself, it also lays the next tracks for itself.

For this train of becoming, the junction of death where the change of tracks takes place is of great importance. Here the present life is abandoned; this is called in Pāli *cuti* (disappearance, death). The demise of the body takes place, and immediately the next life starts, a process called *paṭisandhi* (conception, or beginning of the next life). The moment of *paṭisandhi* is the result of the moment of death; the moment of death creates the moment of conception. Since every death moment creates the next birth moment, death is not only death but birth as well. At this junction, life changes into death and death into birth.

Thus, every life is a preparation for the next death. If one is wise, one will use this life to best advantage and prepare for a good death. The best death is the one that is the last, not a junction but a terminus: the death of an *arahant*. Here there will be no track on which the train can run further. But until such a terminus is reached, one can at least ensure that the next death gives rise to a good birth and that the terminus will be reached in due course. It all depends on us, on our own efforts. We are the makers of our own future; we create our own welfare or misery, as well as our own liberation.

How is it that we are the creators of the tracks that receive the onrushing train of becoming? To answer this question we must understand what *kamma* (action) is.

Mental volition, whether skillful or unskillful, is *kamma*. Whatever wholesome or unwholesome volition arises in the mind becomes the root of all mental, vocal or physical action. Consciousness (*viññāṇa*) arises due to a contact at a sense door, then perception and recognition (*saññā*) evaluate the experience, sensations (*vedanā*) arise, and a kammic reaction (*saṅkhāra*) takes place.

These volitional reactions are of various kinds. Some are like a line drawn on water, disappearing immediately; some like a line drawn on sand, fading away after some interval; and others are like a line chiseled in rock, lasting for a very long time. If the volition is wholesome, the action will be wholesome and the fruits beneficial. But if the volition is unwholesome, the action will be unwholesome and will give fruits of misery.

Not all of these reactions result in a new birth. Some are so shallow that they do not give a significant result. Others are a bit deeper, but will be erased in this lifetime and not carry over into the next. Others, being still deeper, continue with the flow of this life and into the next birth, and can also multiply during this life and the next.

Many *kammas*, however, are *bhāva-kammas* or *bhāva-saṅkhāras*, those that give a new birth, a new life. Each one gives rise to the process of becoming and carries a magnetic force in tune with the vibrations of a particular plane of existence. The vibrations of that *bhāva-kamma* and the vibrations of that *bhāva-loka* (world, plane) attract each other and the two will unite according to universal laws pertaining to forces of *kamma*.

As soon as one of these *bhāva-kammas* is generated, this railway train of becoming gets attracted to one or other of the 31 tracks at the station of death. Actually, these tracks are the 31 planes of existence: the 11 *kāma lokas* (realms of sensuality—the four lower realms of existence, the human world, and six celestial realms), the 16 *rūpa-brahma lokas* (where fine material body remains), and the four *arūpa-brahma lokas* (non-material realms, where only mind exists).

At the last moment of this life a specific *bhāva-saṅkhāra* will arise. This *saṅkhāra*, capable of giving a new birth, will become connected with the vibrations of the related realm of existence. At the instant of death all 31 realms are open. The *saṅkhāra* that arises determines which track the train of existence runs on next. Like shunting a train onto a new track, the force of the *bhāva-kamma* reaction provides a push to the flow of consciousness into the next existence. For example, a *bhāva-kamma* of anger or malice, having heat and agitation as characteristics, will unite with some lower field of existence. Similarly, one like *mettā* (compassionate love), having peaceful and cool vibrations, can only unite with a *brahma-loka*. This is a law of nature, and these laws are so perfectly ordered that there is never any flaw in their operation. It must be understood, of course, that there is no passenger on the train except the force of accumulated *saṅkhāras*.

At the moment of death, generally, some intense *saṅkhāra* will arise. It may be of a wholesome or unwholesome nature. For example, if one has murdered one's father or mother or perhaps some saintly person in this lifetime, then the memory of that event will arise at the moment of death. In the same way, if one has developed some deep meditation practice, a state of mind similar to that will arise.

When there is no such intense *bhāva-kamma*, then a comparatively less intense *kamma* will arise. Whatever memory is awakened will manifest as the *kamma*. One might remember the wholesome *kamma* of giving food to a saintly person, or the unwholesome *kamma* of hurting someone. Reflections on such past *kammas* as these can arise. Otherwise, objects related to that *kamma* might arise: the plate of food that was offered as *dāna* (donation) or the weapon used to harm. These are called the *kamma-nimittas* (signs, images).

Or perhaps a sign or a symbol of the next life might appear. This is called *gati-nimitta* (departing sign). These *nimittas* correspond to the *bhāva-loka* towards which the flow is attracted. It could be the scene of some celestial world, or perhaps of the animal world. The dying person will often experience one of these signs as a precursor, just as a train's headlight illuminates the track ahead. The vibrations of these *nimittas* are identical to the vibrations of the plane of existence of the next birth.

A good Vipassana meditator has the capacity to avoid tracks leading to the lower realms of existence. He or she clearly understands the laws of nature and practices to be ready for death at all times. If one has reached an advanced age, there is all the more reason to remain aware every moment.

What preparations should one undertake? One practices Vipassana by remaining equanimous with whatever sensations arise in the body, thereby breaking the habit of reacting to them. Thus, the mind, which is usually generating new unwholesome *saṅkhāras*, develops the habit of being equanimous.

At the approach of death it is not unlikely that one will experience very unpleasant sensations. Old age, disease and death are *dukkha* (misery), and often, therefore, produce gross unpleasant sensations. If one is not skillful in observing these sensations with equanimity, one will likely react with feelings of fear, anger, sadness, or irritation, providing an opportunity for a *bhāva-saṅkhāra* of like vibration to arise. However, as in the cases of some well-developed meditators, one can work to avoid reacting to these immensely painful sensations by maintaining equanimity at the time of death. Then, even those related *bhāva-saṅkhāras* lying deep in the unconscious will not have an opportunity to arise.

A meditator at the point of death will be fortunate to have close relatives or friends nearby who can practice Vipassana and generate beneficial vibrations of *mettā*, which will create a peaceful Dhamma atmosphere, free from lamenting and gloom.

An ordinary person will usually remain apprehensive, even terror-stricken, at the approach of death, and thus allow a fearful *bhāva-saṅkhāra* to surface. In the same way, grief, sorrow, depression, and other feelings might arise at the thought of separation from loved ones, and the related *saṅkhāra* will come up and dominate the mind. A Vipassana meditator, by observing all sensations with equanimity, weakens these *saṅkhāras* so that they will not arise at the time of death. The real preparation for death is this: developing a habit pattern of repeatedly observing the sensations manifesting in the body and mind with equanimity and with the understanding of *anicca*.

At the time of death this strong habit of equanimity will automatically appear and the train of existence will switch to a track on which it will be possible to practice Vipassana in the new life. In this way one saves oneself from birth in a lower realm and reaches one of the higher ones. Because Vipassana cannot be practiced in the lower realms, this is very important.

At times a non-meditator will attain a favorable rebirth due to the manifestation at the time of death of wholesome *bhāva-saṅkhāras* such as generosity, morality, and other strong, wholesome qualities. But the special achievement of an established Vipassana meditator is to attain an existence where he or she can continue to practice Vipassana. In this way, by slowly decreasing the stock of accumulated *bhāva-saṅkhāras*, one shortens one's journey of becoming and reaches the goal of liberation sooner.

One comes into contact with the Dhamma in this life because of the great merits one has performed in the past. Make this human life successful by practicing Vipassana, so that when death comes the mind is full of equanimity, ensuring well-being for the future.

—S.N. Goenka

Handadāni, bhikkhave, āmantayāmi vo,
vayadhammā saṅkhārā,
appamādena sampādetha.

Now, monks, I exhort you:
All conditioned things have the nature of decay.
Strive on diligently.

—*Mahāparinibbāna Sutta, Dīgha Nikāya* 2.185

Kāmayogena saṃyuttā,
bhāvayogena cūbhayaṃ;
Ditthiyogena saṃyuttā,
avijjāya purakkhatā.
Sattā gacchanti saṃsāraṃ,
jātimaraṇagāmino.

Bound by desire, tied to becoming,
fettered tightly by false opinions,
yoked to ignorance, whirled about:
thus beings wander through *saṃsāra*,
dying only to be born again.

—*Aṅguttara Nikāya* 4.10

Paṭicca Samuppāda

The Law of Dependent Origination

According to the Buddha, our present is the fruit of our past thoughts, words and deeds. Thus, moment by moment our future is shaped by the things we think, say and do in the present. The Buddha's message is profound. Practicing seriously, we realize its unavoidable truth, facing it head-on in our meditations and as we carry out our daily lives. The fact that we are responsible for our future, and that by mastering our minds we can shape it, becomes very clear. Our understanding and acceptance of this law—the law of dependent origination, paṭicca samuppāda*—is what brings us peace of mind and opens the door to our liberation.*

The Buddha spent eons developing the qualities necessary to become fully enlightened—to learn the way out of suffering. Out of deep compassion he offered his discovery to all beings—fearful, angry, greedy, helpless, discouraged, ill, old and dying—so that they too could free themselves from their suffering.

It is a long and difficult path. It can seem so much easier to stick to our old familiar habits of mind, to prefer the pain and suffering of patterns we already know, than to face the discomforts of change that come with training the mind.

Our lives are difficult. There are many days when we feel exhausted and stressed. Rather than face the internal source of our misery, we crave distraction and pleasantness; and so we allow meditation to slip to the bottom of our priority list. Breaking the powerful old habit of craving the pleasant to avoid the unpleasant can seem impossible. But when we are ready to make the effort, the Buddha has provided the perfect tool to make fundamental change.

Following is Goenkaji's explanation of paṭicca samuppāda, *from Day 5 of* The Discourse Summaries.

Obviously the sufferings of life—disease, old age, death, physical and mental pain—are inevitable consequences of being born. But what is the reason for birth? Of course the immediate cause is the physical union of parents, but in a broader perspective birth occurs because of the endless process of becoming in which the entire universe is involved. Even at the time of death the process does not stop: the body continues decaying, disintegrating, while the consciousness becomes connected with another material structure and continues flowing—becoming.

And why this process of becoming? It was clear to the Buddha that the cause is the attachment one develops. Because of attachment one generates strong reactions, *saṅkhāras*, that make a deep impression on the mind. At the end of life, one of these *saṅkhāras* will arise in the mind and give a push so that the flow of consciousness continues.

Now what is the cause of this attachment? The Buddha found that it arises because of the momentary reactions of liking and disliking. Liking develops into great craving; disliking into great aversion, the mirror image of craving; and both turn into attachment.

Why do these momentary reactions of liking and disliking arise? Anyone who observes himself will find that they occur because of bodily sensations. Whenever a pleasant sensation arises, one likes it and wants to retain and multiply it. Whenever an unpleasant sensation arises, one dislikes it and wants to be rid of it.

What causes these sensations? Clearly they occur because of contact between any of the senses and an object of that particular sense: contact of the eye with a vision, of the ear with a sound, of the nose with an odor, of the tongue with a taste, of the body with something tangible, of the mind with a thought. As soon as there is contact, a sensation is bound to arise—pleasant, unpleasant, or neutral.

What is the reason for contact? Obviously, the entire universe is full of sense objects. So long as the six senses—the five physical ones, together with the mind—are functioning, they are bound to encounter their respective objects.

And why do these sense organs exist? It is clear that they are inseparable parts of the flow of mind and matter; they arise as soon as life begins.

Then why does the life-flow, the flow of mind and matter, occur? It is because of the flow of consciousness from moment to moment, from one life to the next.

So why do we have this flow of consciousness? The Buddha found that it arises because of *saṅkhāras*, the mental reactions. Every reaction gives a push to the flow of consciousness; the flow continues because of the impetus given to it by reactions.

And why do reactions occur? He saw that they arise because of ignorance. One does not know what one is doing, does not know how one is reacting, and therefore one keeps generating *saṅkhāras*. As long as there is ignorance, suffering will remain.

The source of the process of suffering, the deepest cause, is ignorance. The chain of events by which one generates mountains of misery for oneself starts from ignorance. If ignorance can be eradicated, suffering will be eradicated.

How can one accomplish this? How can one break the chain? The flow of life, of mind and matter, has already begun. Committing suicide will not solve the problem; it will only create fresh misery. Nor can one destroy the senses without destroying oneself. So long as the senses exist, contact between them and their respective objects is bound to occur, and whenever there is contact a sensation is bound to arise within the body.

And it is here, at the link of sensation, that one can break the chain. Previously, every sensation gave rise to a reaction of liking or disliking that developed into great craving or aversion—great misery. But now, instead of reacting to sensation, you are learning just to observe with equanimity, understanding: "This will also change." In this way sensation gives rise only to wisdom, to the understanding of *anicca*. One stops the turning of the wheel of suffering and starts rotating it in the opposite direction, towards liberation.

Any moment in which one does not generate a new *saṅkhāra*, one of the old ones will rise to the surface of the mind and, along with it, a sensation will start within the body. If one remains equanimous, it passes away and another old reaction arises in its place. One continues to remain equanimous toward the physical sensations and the old *saṅkhāras* continue to arise and pass away, one after another. If, out of ignorance, one reacts to sensations, then one multiplies the *saṅkhāras*, multiplies one's misery. But, if one develops wisdom and does not react to sensations, then one after another, the *saṅkhāras* are eradicated, and misery is eradicated.

The entire path is a way to eradicate misery. By practicing, you will find that you stop tying new knots, and that the old ones are automatically untied. Gradually you will progress toward a stage in which all *saṅkhāras* leading to new birth, and therefore to new suffering, have been eradicated: the stage of total liberation, full enlightenment.

To start the work, it is not necessary that one should first believe in past lives and future lives. In practicing Vipassana the present is most important. Here in the present life, we keep generating *saṅkhāras* and continue to make ourselves miserable. Here and now one must break this habit and start coming out of misery. If you practice, certainly a day will come when you will be able to say that you have eradicated all the old *saṅkhāras*, have stopped generating any new ones, and so have freed yourself from all suffering.

—S.N. Goenka

There is no cause without an effect and there is no effect without a cause. The law of *kamma* is supreme and inevitable. What you have now is the result of what you have done in the past. Until we get rid of the forces of *kamma* which belong to us, once and for all, and enter the supreme *nibbāna*, there is bound to be some trouble or other, here and there, during the remainder of our existence, that we must put up with, using the strength of *anicca*. *Anicca* will surely prevail upon them and you will keep yourself in good stead in spite of all these difficulties. *Anicca* is power. Thorns in the way are inevitable. Make use of the power of *anicca* with diligence and peace will be with you.

—Sayagyi U Ba Khin

Every life is a preparation for the next death. If one is wise, one will use this life to the best advantage and prepare for a good death.

—S.N. Goenka

An Exemplary Death

The following article first appeared in the Vipassana Newsletter, *Dhamma Giri edition in April 1997.*

Dr. Tara Jadhav attended her first Vipassana course in 1986. Her search was over; she had found the pure path of Dhamma and felt no need to explore any other path or technique. With single-minded dedication she began to walk on this path.

Since Tara did not have other responsibilities, she spent most of her time progressing in Dhamma. With her abundant store of *pāramitā* (virtuous qualities), she was able to practice Vipassana easily. Like a fish in water that does not have to be taught to swim, Tara did not have to be given any special training. No doubt she had walked on the path of Dhamma in many previous lives.

She had the technique as well as facilities available for practice, and so she became engrossed in making best use of her time. Since the qualities of *mettā* (loving-kindness) and *karuṇā* (compassion) and a capacity for selfless service were well developed in her, she was appointed an assistant teacher in 1989 and a senior assistant teacher in 1995. In spite of old age she continued to give Dhamma service with great devotion. While guiding students in Vipassana she kept strengthening her *pāramī* of *dāna*.

At the ripe age of 82 she came to Dhamma Giri to take part in a Teachers' Self-Course. On the morning of December 2, 1996, the course started with *ānāpāna*, as usual. She practiced intently throughout the day. After meditating in her cell from 6 to 7 pm she came to the Dhamma hall for the discourse.

At about 7:30 pm, as soon as the discourse began, she knelt with palms and head upon the floor to pay her respects. Once, twice, and after she touched her head to the floor for the third time, she did not raise it again. She breathed her last in the traditional posture of the Dhamma salutation.

Women meditators sitting nearby were surprised to see her bowing thus, because respects are usually paid three times only at the end of a discourse. Why was she offering her respects at the beginning? All three times, while lowering her body, she softly repeated, "*Anicca, anicca, anicca*"—her last words. How could they have known this was to be her final salutation in this life?

All serious meditators are taught that they should never pay respects mechanically. Only when one is equanimous, aware of the impermanence of sensations at the top of the head, is the salutation meaningful. Tara would always bow in this deliberate manner. Her final salutation was all the more deliberate and meaningful.

Tara would tell her Dhamma sisters, "In this twilight of my life I have only one desire: I should give up my body while meditating on this Dhamma land." Her strong Dhamma wish was fulfilled. Becoming established in Vipassana, on the path of liberation, she lived a life of Dhamma and ultimately achieved an exemplary death.

—S.N. Goenka

Questions to Goenkaji I
Supporting Loved Ones at the Time of Death

Student: It seems that *mettā* works, for it is a common experience that when we meet a saintly person we feel better. When we share *mettā* with someone who has died, does this person feel better? Also, there is a belief that, by giving *dāna* in the name of someone who has died, an ancestor or friend, it helps them. Does this belief accord with Dhamma?

Goenkaji: When you say that *mettā* "works," what does this mean? It means that if your mind is pure and you are practicing *mettā*, you are generating vibrations of *mettā*. These vibrations can go anywhere—to this *loka* or that *loka*, to a lower field or a higher field, anywhere. When your *mettā* vibrations come in contact with the being to whom you direct them, he or she feels happy because these are vibrations of Dhamma, of peace, of harmony.

When you donate something in the name of someone who has passed away and say, "May the merit of my donation go to so-and-so," whatever you donated obviously does not go to that person. However, your volition to help this person is one of *mettā*, and those vibrations will flow toward your ancestor or friend and he or she will feel a sense of elation from them. Because these vibrations have a base of Dhamma, something or other will happen to take him or her toward Dhamma in this or a future life. That is how we are helping those who are in lower fields, or even in higher ones.

And now, what do you donate? You donate the best thing you have—your own meditation. Therefore, at the end of your meditation hour or at the end of a meditation course, you remember anyone who is very dear to you or who has passed away, and you say, "I share the merits of my meditation with you." This is your *mettā*. Because you have meditated, the vibrations going to that person are the strong vibrations of

Dhamma. You are sharing your meditation with the person. Naturally it is very helpful.

I worry that those who are getting on in years will keep going through continuous rounds of birth and death because of their attachments—my mother, who is attached to constantly worrying, and a friend very near death who feels that she has been wronged all her life. Can anything be done? Perhaps *mettā*?

Yes. *Mettā*. In addition, keep explaining the law of nature: the more you worry the more you are harming yourself. And there is a technique that can relieve you of this worry.

One cannot say for sure, but they may have a seed of Dhamma from the past. If they get a few words of encouragement, they might be attracted to Dhamma and learn how to relieve themselves of their misery.

If your parents have died, can you benefit them in some way?

Yes, you can. After each of your sittings of meditation, remember them and share your merits with them: "I share with you whatever merits I have gained. May you also feel peaceful and happy." These vibrations will touch them wherever they are. It is not the vibrations themselves that will work some wonder for them; rather, your parents will get attracted toward Dhamma and, who knows, they might find the path. This is the only way: share your merits.

How can family members help at the time of death?

It is always beneficial for the dying person if members of the family are Vipassana meditators. They should make a point of being present so they can meditate and generate *mettā***.** When everybody is calm and quiet, this is wonderfully supportive for the dying person and will help him or her in retaining a calm and quiet mind at the time of death.

Quite often people who are dying in a lot of pain are given strong painkillers such as morphine. For a meditator, is it better to try to work with the pain so that the mind is clear at the moment of death?

It depends on how much the meditator can endure at the time. If, because of pain, the person is reacting with aversion: "Oh, I can't bear this pain!" then you can't be sure that he or she will die with equanimity. So offer some pain medication.

But if the meditator is working with the pain with a balanced mind, wanting to observe things as they are, then don't impose anything. If a meditator is dying and observing calmly without taking medicine, that is his or her choice.

As my mother was dying, she was not happy when we gave her sleeping pills; they made her eyes heavy. Even after taking the sleeping pills, she didn't sleep. She said, "I'm quite happy if I don't get sleep. Why do you want me to sleep?" In her mind, pills were unnecessary and interfered with her meditation.

At the time, there was another old lady next door who was also dying of cancer. The pain for her was unbearable. Her room was on the fourth floor but her cries could be heard on the first. So it all depends on the attitude of the patient.

If the dying person is a meditator, how can we help?

This is wonderful. Meditate with her. Give *mettā*. Listen to some chanting. Because she is a meditator, these things can be done easily.

You can ask her to practice *ānāpāna* or, if she can feel sensations, to stay with sensations. Like this, help her very gently to maintain the awareness of *anicca*. She will be receptive because she is a meditator, so offer her guidance even in meditating. Someone may do that; others can sit and meditate. Listen to some quiet chanting—not too loud; even an experienced meditator may find loud sounds too intense. The *Karaṇīya-mettā Sutta* and the *Maṅgala Sutta* would be beneficial.

Otherwise, remain very quiet. Members of the family, even if not meditators themselves, will know what meditation is. They will know that a Vipassana meditator is dying, and they should abstain from creating an atmosphere of sadness or distress that might tend to make her a little sad as well. One has to be very careful.

If the dying person is not a meditator, can we presume to give Dhamma advice if he has shown no interest in the Dhamma in the past?

No. If he still does not have any faith in Dhamma and you start giving advice, he could generate negativity—"What are these people talking about?"—and it will be harmful. That is why, even in courses, we cannot give Dhamma unless someone requests it. Dhamma should only be given to someone who is receptive. If he is not receptive, that means he is not requesting Dhamma and so we are imposing it. And if, at the time of death, you try to impose something and negativity arises in his mind, then you have started to harm him. However, if you feel that he is positive toward Dhamma, although he has not taken a course, and he can appreciate what you are saying, then you may say a few words about Dhamma.

Can a Vipassana meditator help dying friends and relatives?

If the dying person is a Vipassana meditator, then other meditators can sit nearby and practice Vipassana. This helps to charge the atmosphere with vibrations of purity, love and compassion for this friend or relative. It helps the person retain her purity of mind at the time of death—this has been witnessed many times. If the dying person is not a Vipassana meditator, meditating still helps to purify the atmosphere around her, but obviously it is not as effective as with a meditator.

Jātipi dukkhā,
jarāpi dukkhā,
byādhipi dukkho,
maraṇampi dukkhaṃ,
appiyehi sampayogo dukkho,
piyehi vippayogo dukkho,
yampicchaṃ na labhati tampi dukkhaṃ,
saṇkhittena pañcupādānakkhandhā dukkhā.

Birth is suffering,
aging is suffering,
sickness is suffering,
death is suffering,
association with the unpleasant is suffering,
dissociation from the pleasant is suffering,
not to get what one wants is suffering:
in short, the five aggregates of attachment are suffering.

—*Dhammacakkappavattana Sutta, Saṃyutta Nikāya* 5.1081

Susan Babbitt

Only the Present Moment

Susan Babbitt has been a professor at Queen's University in Kingston, Ontario, Canada since 1990. She attended her first Vipassana course in 2004, and has since served a 10-day course and completed a 20-day course. The first interview took place in 2006, the second in 2007. Susan continues to teach at Queen's, meditates daily and is still cancer-free in 2013.

Virginia: Can you tell us how you found Vipassana, and what your first course was like?

Susan: I was diagnosed with an aggressive form of cancer in August 2003. Until that point in my life I had no experience with illness or medicine. I had not even had the flu. The cancer diagnosis was a brutal assault on my sense of who I was. All of a sudden I was a seriously ill person. I looked for ways to get through this experience. At the beginning something called "guided imagery" was suggested to me, a form of imaginative positive thinking which I tried for several months as a way to escape my fear of what was happening. I used instructional audio tapes.

Then my friend Maureen, who was also going through cancer and who was doing well after treatments, died. I suddenly understood that the only way I would be able to live with cancer was to come to terms with the fact that my existence or non-existence was ultimately out of my control. People were saying to me, "This is not going to happen to you! Your case is different." But I couldn't distinguish myself from her like that. I knew that what happened to her could happen to me. The "positive thinking" approach leads one to believe that one has some control, and of course one does have *some* control, but the final result is not under my control.

It was clear to me that I had to be able to look at what was happening to me for what it was, to accept that death was indeed possible. I decided that I wanted to be able to expect the worst-case scenario, and to live with it; that is, to live my life with awareness of what could very well happen to me. Practically, this seemed the most reasonable thing to do. At that time I knew nothing about meditation or Vipassana. I *had* read here and there, in oncology books, that meditation is a good thing for cancer patients to learn. But I had no idea how to meditate, and when I tried to do it I failed.

Shortly after Maureen's death the doctors recommended that I undergo chemotherapy therapy, which I had not expected. I hated the idea of chemotherapy therapy. I had had surgery on my leg followed by radiation. These I could handle, but everything about chemotherapy was awful to me—the idea that I would feel sick, that I would look sick, that everybody would know I was sick, that it was going to be from March to August, for the whole spring and summer of 2004, five months long. I was angry and resentful, and I thought, "How am I going to get through five months?"

I didn't want to spend those months angry and resentful so I went to the social worker at the Kingston Regional Cancer Centre and asked, "What tools do you have to offer?" She gave me a book on Buddhism that I started to read. It had to do with compassion and loving-kindness, but after about four chapters I returned it. I asked, "How does this help me, practically, to get through five months of chemotherapy?" I was frustrated that there was no practical guidance.

I kept thinking about meditation, however, and remembered this Vipassana course I had heard about. I thought, well, if I'm going to learn how to meditate, I might as well go all the way; you can only learn meditation by doing it.

I found an application form and signed up. I had no idea what the course was about, except that it was about meditation. So I committed myself to the 10 days from March 24 to April 4, 2004, starting just a few days after the first chemotherapy treatment.

The course was extremely difficult for me, and for the first three days I questioned what I was doing there. On the fourth day, when Vipassana was taught, I became more interested. I had understood somehow, when Maureen died, that I wanted to be able to see things as they are, to be able to look at the real probability of death, and to live my life in the face of it. I didn't want to be trying to make things look better than they might be—ever hoping desperately for good news, ever fearful of the bad. I had decided that I couldn't live my life always looking for ways to separate myself from those getting the bad news.

With cancer, at least the kind I had, there's no returning to your old life. You have to go for a CT scan every few months, and each time you go there is a real possibility of bad news. I didn't want to lose my life to fear. I understood also that if I didn't confront and accept the real possibility of death, fear would always be lurking over me, ready to descend and debilitate me at every indication that things were not going the way I wanted. I had decided that I wanted to be able to confront my reality and accept it for what it was, to live with it.

So I was surprised to learn that Vipassana is precisely the practice of looking at your reality just as it is, not as you want it to be. It is the systematic, hour-after-hour observation of your entire physical and mental experience. You incrementally gain thereby an experiential understanding of the real nature of your existence, which is, after all, impermanent. There is no turning of bad things into good things, as so many seem to try to do with disease and death. Instead, you look at things the way they are, which is the way of the entire universe, constantly changing. And when you gain such awareness, which must be experiential, meaning awareness that is felt, it makes no sense to identify yourself with either the good or the bad, and therefore to become debilitated by either desperate hope or by desperate fear.

It is strange that I somehow realized, intuitively, that I could not be free from the fear of disease and death unless I could see my experience of cancer in the worst possible way, and live with that. I don't mean just to tolerate it, but to live in the face of that reality with full awareness of the precarious nature of my existence, even seeing the beauty of that ever-changing mysterious nature.

I learned at the Vipassana course that this is what the Buddha taught, not a religion, but a practical technique of mental discipline, cultivating freedom from the dominating expectations that lead us to think life should be a certain way—expectations that make us miserable when they fail, as they almost certainly do.

Of course I was still angry about the cancer because cancer wasn't supposed to happen to me. Yet it *was* happening to me, and I knew that I could not make it go away. I knew also that I had to get out of the grip of unfounded expectations about how my life should be and move forward with open eyes. The simple practice of focusing my mind on the reality of my own bodily existence and becoming aware of its nature—such a simple idea—was, I discovered, the tool that I needed to go through chemotherapy, and much more.

One thing in particular that really appealed to me about the practice of Vipassana, which I learned at that first course, was that it was entirely practical. I did not have to believe in any unseen entities or forces, or depend on anyone or anything outside of myself: no symbols, special dress, or rites or rituals. Vipassana is a practical tool for training the mind. I was well aware of how much time I had lost from my life when my mind was out of control, somewhere else, reliving old dramas or spinning uselessly around the same old problems and fears. Vipassana teaches control of the mind so that we can live entirely in our world as it is, instead of forever running away into imagination or resentment.

So Vipassana helped me get through the awful process of chemotherapy and its consequences. I did not have to try to see chemotherapy as a good thing. Indeed, I looked at that chemotherapy experience as unacceptable. But I could *also* look at it objectively to some extent and say, "This is what is happening now." I accepted it as my reality at this moment, as it is, and would start again from there without regret or disappointment.

After the cancer treatments were over I went for a second Vipassana course at the end of 2004. Although I was not then dealing with cancer, I had other things to deal with. The second course was almost harder than the first, except that this time I understood why I was doing what I was doing. The course was painful, physically. I didn't need to talk to the teacher because I knew what I had to do and I knew what he would tell me. I just looked at that pain over and over again and practiced equanimity.

At the end of the course, the teacher called me for a conversation and said, “You sat through it, you accepted it with awareness; that is all you can do. Your job is to be aware, even when the experience is unpleasant.” That course was important because I realized I had a lot of other things to deal with besides cancer. Cancer was only one thing in my life, and maybe not even the most important source of negativity, so I was motivated to keep up the practice.

What happened after your second course?

By the summer of 2005 my life was getting back to normal. I had regained the use of my leg and had fully returned to work. I was getting ready for my sabbatical when, in September, my leg became stiffer. On the first of October, which was actually the beginning of a three-month sabbatical, I found another lump on my leg. I knew even before the doctors did that it was recurrent cancer. The whole month of October was extremely difficult because I knew the cancer was back, but I didn't know whether it had gone anywhere else. Moreover, the doctors hadn't confirmed that it was back and I couldn't really tell people about it. They couldn't do the CT scan, to see if it had spread, until October 28.

Those four weeks were hell. I knew the cancer was back but I didn't know the extent of it. I was going to have to go through the whole thing again. My career would again be interrupted and I was sure that, this time, I would lose my leg. What do you do with all these thoughts? All you have is your mind, and the fears go round and round. Where do you go to flee from your mind? I thought that if I hadn't learned meditation I would've gone crazy. I could easily have fallen into a deep pit of despair and nobody would have blamed me, for it would have been completely reasonable.

Instead, I would sit amid those strong debilitating emotions, concentrate my mind, and patiently observe sensations, sometimes most of the night, and eventually the fears would loosen their hold. I found that I could coexist with the fears and grief, like looking straight into darkness, and eventually feel some peace knowing that it had to be this way, at least for now. I did manage to function that month. I helped my mother prepare for her trip to Ireland, and I did other things that I had to do, more or less normally.

I looked for a way to think about the possibility of death. Somebody gave me a book by a Vietnamese Buddhist monk. His ideas about life and death made sense to me, suggesting that we are like waves in the sea. Waves arise and disappear but the sea remains. Everybody has a right to live life as a wave but we also need to live our life as water. Life doesn't go away; it just changes form, like the waters of the ocean, constantly moving. I also read the Persian poet Rumi who has beautiful things to say about acceptance. But when October 28 came around, I found that all these nice ideas did nothing to alleviate the grip of the terror I was feeling about the CT scan that might tell me the cancer had spread.

So that day, when I got ready for the appointment, I found myself going back to the practice of Vipassana, which is the simple experience of the rising and passing away of all sensory aspects of the entire bodily structure. In Vipassana you experience, by observing sensations, the real nature of all existence—dynamic, temporary, but real. When you experience your reality like that, how can you be afraid? For when you are aware of yourself as an integral part of larger, constantly unfolding natural phenomena, uncertainty is not so threatening and scary. It is now expected, not foreign, and therefore easier to live through. I was calm when I went to the hospital and even talked to a student about her thesis as I waited for the scan. As it turned out, I got good news that day.

It struck me that I hadn't thought much before about the difference between intellectual and experiential understanding. I had been trying to prepare myself for bad news by looking for ideas. I discovered in the end that all those useful ideas I had gathered had given me some intellectual understanding but did not alleviate the fears. Intellectual understanding frequently is not real understanding. In the end I had to feel the truth about life and death through awareness of sensations. It was practical, felt awareness, not intellectual truths, that helped me get through that day.

Did that realization give you more confidence in your practice?

Yes, it did. I realized that my mistake had been to look for a theoretical understanding of death, and no merely intellectual understanding of death was going to help me confront it. We all know, intellectually, that we can die at any moment, but we don't believe that this truth actually applies to us. It is abstract. We believe it, but we don't *feel* the truth of what we believe, and it plays no real role in how we live our lives. It is a truth that does not matter to our lives. Meditation is the experience, moment after moment, hour after hour, of the uncertain nature of existence; and, in undergoing such an experience, death cannot be abstract, for its reality is there in each moment of real awareness.

I began radiation treatments at Princess Margaret Hospital in Toronto. I stayed at the hospital lodge for five weeks, going twice a day to the hospital for this very painful radiation. I didn't feel like I had any kind of balance during this time. I was in a lot of pain and I didn't like being away from home. I felt bad physically and I was losing hope. It's easy to lose hope when physically you feel terrible.

At that time I didn't have much peace of mind, but I remembered what one of my Vipassana instructors had told me: If you can't maintain your balance of mind, just be aware that you don't have balance of mind and you'll *still* keep moving ahead. This is a powerful part of the Buddha's teaching. It is not about being immediately successful. When things are going badly, I can still look at my reality as it is, aware of its ultimately impermanent nature, and start again from there.

The surgery to remove the tumor and save my leg was 13 hours long and the recovery was difficult. Finally I went home and began physiotherapy. It was now April 2006. The cancer was gone, spring had arrived, and I was becoming mobile again. But just one week after I left the hospital they told me the cancer was in my lungs. This was devastating news because when cancer has metastasized the prognosis is poor. They told me I had a 20 percent chance of living another five years, and that, of course, was hard to hear.

I was upset about this for three or four days and then, as in October 2005, I realized that I had to look at the fear and disappointment, and wait. Again, I was so thankful that I had a tool to deal with this, to deal with my mind and the grip of terror. People try to be helpful in such situations, but in the end you're left with your mind. You're alone with uncertainty and anguish. I would sit, hour after hour, and finally I found that I could be at peace with it. I could talk about the probability of death and even joke about it, which was surprising.

As I accepted the situation I realized that what was hard about the idea of dying was not that I would die soon, at 53 rather than 83 as I had always expected, but that I would die *at all*. It was not premature death that was hard, but death itself. I realized it was *death* that I thought could never happen to me, not premature death, or death by cancer.

One of the ideas that I had relied upon to try to accept death was something that Albert Einstein said: We fear death because we cling to an idea of ourselves as discrete individuals, but if we can see ourselves as part of the unfolding of the universe, which is beautiful in its complexity and mystery, we won't be so fearful. This is what meditation allows me to do experientially, to understand myself as part of the unfolding of the universe, which is beautiful in its mystery. What we're doing in meditation is experiencing, hour by hour, the rising and passing away, the impermanence, of all the sensations in the body. My reality, my entire physical and mental structure, is impermanent, changing from moment to moment, precisely as is the whole universe. Everything I'm part of is constantly changing too, moment to moment, and moreover is beautiful because of it. At the end of his life Einstein said that death had to be approached elegantly, that is, without fear—that we can't run away from it. It's the nature of our existence that we each are an integral part of the mysterious unfolding of the universe.

It has been through the practice of meditation that I realized that I can experience myself as part of this mysterious and complex unfolding of the universe. I now think that death won't be so difficult if I can remain constantly aware of the ever-changing nature of my entire physical and mental structure. This takes practice. Thomas Merton said, "In silence is the victory over death." He meant mental silence. In silence is the victory over death because it's when your mind is quiet that you can appreciate the nature of your existence. In those moments, fear loses its grip.

You have time left in your life, but you don't know how much; you have a goal to teach again as a philosopher. Has your presentation to students changed due to your experience?

The philosophical tradition that we teach in universities in Canada and the U.S. does not give importance to experiential understanding. It's not that there aren't philosophers who have talked about it, but we primarily teach people to analyze, to distinguish concepts, to define their terms clearly, to make and refute arguments. If the concept of experiential understanding exists in Western philosophical traditions, it is not prominent. I would like to use the two courses that I'm teaching to help students see the importance of experiential understanding.

Thomas Merton said that the greatest test of our freedom is death. We'll all die sometime, but the approach we take toward death can make death a choice for life, not death. I'm never going to be happy about my death, but I can still be free while not happy. I can be free to look at that unhappiness and accept it, be at peace with it.

I'm in the position now of trying to live my life with death staring me in the face every day. I wake up to the reality that my life might end very soon, and I have realized that I can live with this if I can remain aware of the nature of my existence. I can live free from fear if I rely not merely on my intellectual understanding but on the experiential, on truths that are felt.

So, I would like to challenge my students to think about freedom and what it requires, and to get them to see that they must also seek the wisdom that is the result of what is lived. Philosophy is the love of wisdom. That is what the word means. But wisdom is acquired through experience. I'm afraid that what we teach is not even philosophy. It is not about wisdom. We don't teach people to live, to experience the truth of their lives. Instead, we teach them to watch themselves live, and to be content with being able to tell a good story, an intelligent, logically consistent story about who they are and what they have done. I would like to ask students to think about why our intellectual resources are so often useless for understanding something like death, which is also understanding existence, and what it means to be free.

Follow-up interview, December 2007

We last talked in the late spring of 2006. You ended up having more surgery that year and again in 2007. How did you get through that and back to teaching—and what happened afterward?

In April 2006 I learned that the cancer had spread and that my prognosis was poor, but the doctors did not tell me the disease was incurable. In a case of sarcoma, they treat lung metastases aggressively with surgery and some people do survive. But they said my chances were slim. They did the first lung surgery in May 2006 and removed seven malignant tumors. Then, almost immediately after, in June, there were more "nodules" showing in the scan. They did not recommend surgery again that summer so I returned to teaching in the fall.

I was happy to go back to teaching, although I was well aware of the cancer. A friend and colleague asked me recently why I wanted to go back to teaching, knowing, as I did, that my life would likely end soon. I told her that indeed there had been a time in the summer of 2006 when I thought that perhaps I should do something special with the rest of my now shortened life—maybe travel to some new places or write some important book. But when I reflected upon this, the idea struck me as ridiculous. I did not regret losing my life because of the things I might have done or accomplished, had I lived. I regretted losing my life because of life itself, the moment-by-moment experience of it.

I had once thought interesting the question of what I would do if I knew I had only months to live. But when I ended up in that situation, there was no such question: All I wanted to do were the ordinary everyday things that I had always done. I can't say that I came to this conclusion because of the practice of Vipassana, for I know other cancer patients who have come to the same conclusion without meditation. Yet I do think it a result of practicing Vipassana that this truth was so easy to accept and to apply to what was left of my life. And I am certain that it was because of Vipassana that there was no sense whatsoever of sadness about this. There's something tempting in the idea that death should be dramatic, and that something *important* should be done or said to mark the event, as if to underline the "meaning" of it all. Yet all I wanted for whatever was left of my very ordinary life was the quiet simple awareness of its most mundane aspects—no extra fun or excitement, and certainly no drama or sentimentality. What is ordinary is all the more miraculous when death is close. This is a truth I had already experienced through my practice of Vipassana.

So I went back to teaching and found it somehow easy in a way that it had not been before. I was doing what I had to do, what I had always done, and what I believed in, but I was not concerned about the importance of it. This is not to say that it wasn't important. What I was doing and teaching was important and meaningful to me in the way it had always been, but it was not *important* that it was important and meaningful. What this means is that I found that I was living my life without watching myself live my life, without telling myself mental stories about how and why I was living my life. Somehow my relations with students were much easier and more direct.

I finished that fall term and had more operations in the winter of 2006–07. It was a tough time because one of the surgical procedures went wrong and I ended up with chronic pain and less mobility. But by autumn I had returned to teaching, again wondering whether I'd finish the term.

Then, in the middle of last October, almost immediately after I had been told by the oncologist that everything was OK, I got news that there was a large tumor near my heart. The news had come in a radiologist's report. They had missed it in two previous scans. A few weeks later the doctors informed me that the tumor was inoperable but they could try some chemotherapy—however it would be only palliative, that is, it would be to stave off the symptoms and perhaps give me more time. That was the news I received in early November 2007.

When the doctor told you that he could offer only palliative treatment, what did you feel then? What were your expectations?

I talked to the oncologist by phone on the evening of November 5, and he told me then that I would probably live another three to six months if the chemotherapy did not work—and there was not much chance that it would. I was surprised that I was able to converse so calmly with him. I tried to get as much information as I could and also complained about the fact that the tumor had been missed by the radiologist in August. I told him too that I appreciated that he had saved my leg even though it now seemed like I wouldn't survive after all.

When I finished the conversation I phoned my mother and gave her the news, calmly, although this was hard for her. Then I sat in my living room in the dark for several hours and quietly and dispassionately watched feelings of fear, despair, sadness, and anxiety. I had hoped to survive; now I would not. I could already feel the tumor pressing on my esophagus and so I expected that it would eventually choke me. I experienced a lot of anxiety about the process of death and what I had to do to prepare for it. I just watched these feelings, and after a long time I felt somehow comforted, for what I was seeing and accepting at that moment was just the nature of our human reality—utter insecurity and aloneness, with nothing to hang onto but the present moment. I had a sense of freedom and peace that night, feeling that I was then at the real center of my life, fully in touch with the entirely uncertain reality of my existence.

I still had almost half the semester ahead of me. But perhaps because I had spent so much time in meditation, being aware of what's happening in my body and understanding that everything in the universe is constantly changing, dying, and coming back to life, the news that I might not be alive in three months seemed almost irrelevant. Of course it was shocking, and hard. But I had, in some small way at least, become used to the idea that I only ever have the present, and everybody else only has the present too.

As in 2006, I had this thought, momentarily, that perhaps, having just three months or so to live, I should say something important to the students, or do something special. It also struck me, though, that the best thing I could offer to them was an example. They'd know in a few months, if I died, what I had been living with, and I would have shown them that it is possible to live normally with the reality of death, which we all must do if we are not to lose our lives to fear. I didn't want to give them, or anyone else, mere words. Somehow that seemed wrong. Words had not helped me face the fear of death, nor live with it, to the extent that I did, in peace. It was the practice of Vipassana, which is calmly and quietly seeing things as they are, that had helped me live with death so near. So I didn't tell the students or my colleagues about my situation. If I had, I would not have been able to keep doing things normally as before, which is what I most wanted.

Nothing much changed in my life after I received that grave news. I had to teach my students and I found that I could. Occasionally it felt strange talking to students or listening to them do their presentations musing, "I will soon be dead, yet I'm sitting here listening to these presentations." Then I would think, "But it is irrelevant, really irrelevant, because we are all in this situation. I have this moment and only this moment, and they also have this moment and only this moment. They don't believe it, and they wouldn't believe it if I told them, but this is the reality we all share."

I felt that I was lucky to have had a year and a half expecting this sort of situation. This is not to say that I was negative and without hope, but rather that I had decided that I could live better with the disease, practically, if I expected the worst and lived with it—that is, if I expected death and learned to live normally with that expectation. When I began practicing Vipassana, I learned that this is just how anyone should live because this is the essential nature of our very fragile and precarious existence.

As a result of three years of Vipassana practice it was clear to me that all anyone has in her or his life are the ordinary simple everyday activities of the present, and the awareness of them. Of course, it is easy to say this, and many people do say this, as I did in the past. But since very few people pursue the quietness of mind that allows real awareness of the moment, many people just *say* this and at the same time lose their lives. As the Cuban philosopher José Martí warned, we have to work hard to claim our existence and, if we do *not*, our life will go by like the Guadiana River (in Spain) that flows quickly, silently, and invisibly beneath the earth, so that we barely even notice its passing.

Instead of saying *my* awareness, you seem now to be talking about *the* awareness, because what you are experiencing is that equanimous sense of the "I" as momentary, connecting to the next momentary "I" in the next present moment and the next present moment.

Maybe this is the most powerful thing that happens when one practices meditation daily: the ego falls away without one noticing it. In fact, it seems to be part of the nature of the experience of losing ego and becoming more aware of the present as a result, that no one notices it. I think this is one way that people get it wrong about mindfulness, which is a popular topic now. They make such an effort to be mindful of what they are doing that they are concentrating more on the effort they are making. But the ancient Chinese philosopher Chuang Tzu said that when the shoe fits, we don't notice it. When you practice meditation day after day your mind becomes quieter and, as a result, more observant, and you become less concerned with what it means to be mindful. You just are. And when you are in fact mindful, aware of the present moment, you are not concerned about your "self" because the self falls away. It has to.

But this only happens with practice, over time, a lot of time. Without that slow patient process of loss of ego, you can't ever really live in the present because you're constantly concerned with what it means—mostly for yourself—to practice awareness of the present moment. When you really understand that your life only has meaning in the present, those questions about self-importance don't matter, and you become free from debilitating, mostly fearful, self-analysis. If the effort toward mindfulness is a concern for self, then it is really not mindfulness at all, at least not in the liberating sense that the Buddha taught.

We're all wrapped up in this concept of ego, this illusion of "I." If the need to control is a result of the ego idea trying to hold on, do you feel this need fades as the ego fades? If control dissolves, how does this help deepen your equanimity, your sense of peace?

The prospect of death is very humbling, because when you lose your life and your future, you lose control. When I learned about the inoperable tumor, I also learned that it was there in the August report but that the radiologist had missed it. The doctors could have seen that tumor in August, maybe even in June, but they didn't. I told the oncologist that this error needed to be addressed, but I didn't really feel a lot of on going anger or resentment about it. I let it go.

No great anger that they missed the tumor in June?

I told the oncologist that I didn't care about pursuing this question but someone should care because someone screwed up and I was losing my life. He said, "You should raise it, because it goes further if the patient raises it." "Well," I replied, "I'd have to be stupid to spend the last months of my life doing that. You just informed me I'm going to die. Why would I want to go chasing the guy who screwed up? You should do that. It's your job. It's your hospital." After that I never thought about it again.

Was that loss of control, or loss of ego?

I just wanted to see that it got corrected so that it didn't happen to anyone else. But I was surprised that I didn't care more because that error was extremely costly to me. Maybe they could have saved my life if they'd seen the tumor back in June or in August.

What about the teaching of the Buddha that we alone are completely responsible for what we've done in the past; that what happened in the past conditions what happens in the present?

Well, I always remember that Goenkaji said we have responsibility for just the present moment. Occasionally I wonder what I did in the past to have brought all this upon myself—four years of cancer treatment—but then I remember that I have responsibility for only what's happening now, and that's enough. I have to practice that part of it. That's the part that frees me from the bondage of resentment and anger. On some level I hate all this stuff—pain, doctors' appointments, medications, treatments, IV lines, nursing care, dependence, being in the hospital again and again. I was so healthy, strong, and athletic before this. It would be easy, perhaps even reasonable, to fall into a pit of resentment.

When you indulge in that resentment, you've lost the present moment.

Yes. Vipassana is a very important tool. I just start looking at the breath. All those nights in the hospital—hot, stuffy, claustrophobic—there's nothing to like about it. But you concentrate on breathing and you're there in the moment, and eventually it's over. And then you leave until the next time. But I have to practice it, like anything else.

You might have two months left; you might have two years, or more. During that time, what is the most important thing for you to do in order to finish things well?

I believe very much in simplicity and silence, by which I mean silence of the mind. I don't find myself thinking very much about how things will be until I die. I trust what Goenkaji says, that if you practice daily, in the end you'll have the resources to deal with it. I know from talking to people who work in palliative medicine that the process of dying can unfold in many ways. So I just want to live each moment, as much as possible, with peace and awareness. And I want that to be easy, like a shoe that fits. I know that that only happens with mental discipline built up through the wonderful daily practice of meditation. I'm grateful to have learned the miracle of silence, not the exterior silence that can be experienced even in agitation, but interior silence that is freedom from mental conversations rooted in fear and self-importance, robbing you of sensitivity to the here and now.

I can't really think past January, a few weeks from now, when I'll go for the next chemotherapy treatment. The last time I went to the hospital the doctor told me that the tumor had grown and he was going to send me home without any more treatments. I sat alone in the hospital after one chemotherapy treatment—my ride had left thinking I was supposed to be there for four days of treatment—and he was telling me that the thing hadn't shrunk, or even stabilized, but that it was larger. I was surprised that I just listened to what he said and was not particularly agitated. I didn't expect bad news that day, and this was really bad news. As it turned out—four hours later—the oncologist ordered another scan and determined that, although the tumor was larger, it had lost 75 per cent of its mass, so he decided to continue the chemotherapy. That was another hard day. The only way to get through these things is to practice staying right there in the present moment.

You were surprised but you didn't react. Was some part of your mind equanimously watching sensations because you'd trained yourself to do so?

Perhaps. I can imagine people falling apart. I can easily imagine myself falling apart. This was the worst news. They had said there was a small chance that the chemotherapy would work and now the doctor was saying that that small chance didn't exist, it wasn't happening.

You said that you didn't want this period of your life, however long it is, to be taken from you, that you want to live each present moment. Can you put this idea into words once more?

Yes, that's true. It's a practical problem. I don't want to lose whatever is left of my life to fear, anger, resentment, and regret. And the only way I can do that is to look at what's happening right now and not at what I would like to be happening—to see things as they are and to be free from expectations about how things ought to be.

Your freedom comes from being in the present moment and not reacting?

Yes. I know now that you have to feel the truth of this idea. People talk so much now about mindfulness. It's trendy. But it's all about self-importance. *I* am aware. *I* am in the present. When you really are aware of yourself in the present, you are not aware that you are aware. You don't think about that awareness itself. What you are aware of is the arising and passing away of each moment in time. You cannot at the same time be stuck on yourself and your significance, because that too is arising and passing away, forever. The nature of our existence is, after all, impermanent. We all know this and say it again and again, but when you feel this truth at each moment in time you also lose the concern for self. It's not a big deal. It's a simple idea, but at the same time very hard. Whether I'm going to be dead soon or whether I'm not going to be dead soon, I really have only this, the present moment.

Kṣhaṇa kṣhaṇa kṣhaṇa kṣhaṇa bītate,
jīvana bītā jāya.
Kṣhaṇa kṣhaṇa kā upayoga kara,
bītā kṣhaṇa nā āya.

Moment after moment after moment,
life keeps slipping by.
Make use of every moment;
the moment past will never come again.

—Hindi *doha*, S.N. Goenka

Kamma—the Real Inheritance

Experiential wisdom that comes from meditation practice confirms that we alone are solely responsible for who and what we are. We cannot escape this law of nature. This understanding strengthens our desire to practice and serve Dhamma. It has a strong driving power that supports us in the dark moments of meditation or at times when we are tired and the mundane world seems to be winning us over.

As plants from sprouted seeds eventually bear more such seeds in future, in our daily lives momentary thoughts, words, and deeds sooner or later give their results accordingly. That future might be bright or dark. If in the present we make right efforts toward wholesomeness, awareness, and equanimity, the future becomes brighter. If through ignorance we react with craving and aversion, the future will be fraught with darkness.

The teachings of the Buddha show us how to develop the awareness of anicca *and the habit pattern of equanimity in the face of both pleasant and unpleasant sensations. Knowing that this and only this is what dissolves the old habit patterns that make life so hard for us and for those around us is a supreme wisdom. This is what draws us out of misery and towards* nibbāna. *This is why we practice. If in the present we are watchful, prudent and diligent, we can bring to our futures a profound change for the better.*

During the final discourse given in all long Vipassana courses, Goenkaji elaborates on the following exhortation of the Buddha. This article, excerpted from that discourse, was published in the June 1995 Vipassana Newsletter.

Kammassakā, bhikkhave,
sattā kammadāyādā kammayonī
kammabandhū kammapaṭisaraṇā.
yaṃ kammaṃ karonti—kalyāṇaṃ vā pāpakaṃ vā—
tassa dāyādā bhāvanti.

O meditators, beings are the owners of their deeds,
the heirs of their deeds, born of their deeds,
kin to their deeds; their deeds are their refuge.
Whatever actions they perform, whether good or evil,
such will be their inheritance.

—*Aṅguttara Nikāya* 10.216

Kammassakā: O meditators, beings are the owners of their deeds.

The law of *paṭicca samuppāda* (dependent origination) is the universal law of cause and effect: As the action is, so the result will be. Mental volition is the driving force for action, vocal or physical. If this driving force is unwholesome, the vocal and physical actions will be unwholesome; if the seeds are unwholesome, then the fruits are bound to be unwholesome. But if this driving force is wholesome, then the results of the actions are bound to be wholesome. For a Vipassana student who develops the ability to observe this law at the level of direct experience, the answer to the question "Who am I?" becomes clear. You are nothing but the sum total of your *kamma*, your *saṅkhāras*. All your accumulated actions together equal "I" at the conventional level.

Kamma dāyādā: heirs of their deeds.

In the worldly, conventional sense one says, "I received this inheritance from my mother or my father or my elders," and yes, at the apparent level this is true. But what is one's real inheritance? *Kamma dāyādā*. One inherits one's own *kamma*, the results, the fruits of one's own *kamma*. Whatever you are now, the present reality of this mind-matter structure is nothing but the result, the sum total, of your own accumulated past *kamma*. The experience of the present moment is the sum total of all that is acquired, inherited—*kamma dāyādā*.

Kammayonī: born of their deeds.

One says, "I am the product of a womb; I have come out of the womb of my mother"—but this is only apparent truth. Actually, your birth is because of your past *kamma*. You come from the womb of your own *kamma*. As you start understanding Dhamma in a deeper and more experiential manner, you realize this. This is *kammayonī*, the womb that every moment produces the fruit of accumulated *kamma*.

Kammabandhū: kin to their deeds.

No one else is your relative—not your father, your mother, your brother, nor your sister. In the worldly way we say, "This is my brother, my relative, or my near or dear one; they are so close to me." Actually, no one is close to you; no one can accompany you or help you when the time comes. When you die, nothing accompanies you but your *kamma*. Those whom you call your relatives remain here, but your *kamma* continues to follow you from one life to another. You are not in possession of anything but your own *kamma*. It is your only kin and companion.

Kamma paṭisaraṅā: their deeds are their refuge

Refuge is only in one's own *kamma*. Wholesome *kamma* provides a refuge; unwholesome *kamma* produces more suffering. No other being can give you refuge. When you say "*Buddhaṃ saraṅaṃ gacchāmi*" (I take refuge in the Buddha), you understand fully well that a person by the name of Gotama, who became the Buddha, cannot give you refuge. Your own *kamma* gives you refuge. Nobody can protect you, not even a buddha. Refuge in the Buddha is refuge in the quality of the Buddha: the enlightenment, the teaching that he gave. By following the teaching, you can develop enlightenment within you. And the enlightenment that you develop within you, that is your wholesome *kamma*. This alone will give you refuge; this alone will give you protection.

Yaṃ kammaṃ karonti—kalyāṇam vā pāpakaṃ vā tassa—dāyādā bhāvanti: whatever actions they perform, whether good or evil, such will be their inheritance.

This should become clear to one who is on the path. This law of nature should become very clear. Then you will become inspired to take responsibility for your own *kamma*. Remain alert and on guard each moment so that every action, physical or mental, is wholesome. You will not be perfect, but keep trying. You may fall down, but see how quickly you can get up. With renewed determination, renewed inspiration, and renewed courage, get up and try again. This is how you become strong in Dhamma.

—S.N. Goenka

Na santi puttā tāṇāya,
na pitā nāpi bandhavā;
antakenādhipannassa,
natthi ñātīsu tāṇatā.

Etamatthavasaṃ ñatvā,
paṇḍito sīlasaṃvuto
nibbānagamanaṃ maggaṃ,
khippameva visodhaye.

Sons are no protection,
neither father nor kinsfolk;
when assailed by death,
there's no protection among kin.

Perceiving thus,
the wise and self-restrained
quickly clear the path
that leads to *nibbāna*.

—*Dhammapada* 20.288-289

Atītaṃ nānvāgameyya, nappaṭikaṅkhe anāgataṃ;
yadatītaṃ pahīnaṃ taṃ, appattañca anāgataṃ.
Paccuppannañca yo dhammaṃ, tattha tattha vipassati;
asaṃhīraṃ asaṃkuppaṃ, taṃ vidvāmanubrūhaye.

Ajjeva kiccamātappaṃ ko jaññā maraṇaṃ suve;
Na hi no saṅgaraṃ tena mahāsenena maccunā.
Evaṃ vihāriṃ ātāpiṃ, ahorattamatanditaṃ;
taṃ ve bhaddekaratto'ti
santo ācikkhate muni.

One should not linger on the past nor yearn for what is yet to come.
The past is left behind, the future out of reach.
But in the present he observes with insight each phenomenon,
immovable, unshakable. Let the wise practice this.

Today, strive at the task. Tomorrow death may come—who knows?
We can have no truce with death and his mighty horde.
Thus practicing ardently, tireless by day and night;
for such a person, even one night is auspicious,
says the Tranquil Sage.

— *Bhaddekarattasuttaṃ, Majjhimanikāya,*
Uparipaṇṇāsapāḷi, Vibhaṅgavaggo

Rodney Bernier
1944–2009

Smiling All the Way to Death

Rodney Bernier was born in 1944 in eastern Canada. His parents' relationship collapsed when he was a young child and he ended up in an orphanage in England, with insufficient food and often bullied. Illiterate and with no skills, he left the orphanage while a young teenager and found work as a laborer. He fought drug addiction, which he eventually overcame. Considering the harshness of his early years, Rodney's playful joviality, delightful sense of humor, and characteristically good-hearted nature were all the more extraordinary.

He traveled to India and in 1973 applied for a 10-day Vipassana meditation course with Goenkaji in Bombay. That first course had a powerful impact and he immediately attended two more. By the end of the second course, at only 28 years of age, he made a commitment to himself to practice Vipassana for the rest of his life. Meditation and the teaching of the Buddha became his cornerstones. One aspect of the practice, especially, resonated deeply: mettā.

Rodney eventually settled in British Columbia where he became a legendary tree planter, planting more than one million trees in 25 years. In middle age he decided to return to school to learn to read and write, and during this time he sat and served many Vipassana courses, including 30- and 45-day courses. He supported the local meditation community in Vancouver by hosting weekly group sittings and eventually, for almost three decades, daily 5 pm group sittings.

In May 2009 Rodney was diagnosed with metastasized liver cancer. He remained at home, but by July the tumors had spread to his spinal cord and he was unable to walk. He was hospitalized for the remaining five weeks of his life.

Rodney recognized when the end was near. He looked up at the pictures of Goenkaji by his bed and drew his hands together in a gesture of deep respect for his teacher. A friend sitting next to him asked if he wanted his hand held. Rodney indicated no; it was time to focus inwardly and prepare. At 5 pm he and his fellow meditators had their customary afternoon group sitting. Although he was awake throughout, as the sitting ended he slipped into a coma. For several hours a few Dhamma friends meditated with him as a recording of Goenkaji's chanting played quietly. Rodney died in the early morning hours of August 13, 2009. A profound sense of calm and peace enveloped everyone present.

During his final weeks some meditators wondered whether Rodney's seemingly extraordinary attitude toward death was merely bravado masking deeper fears; however, he continued to radiate joy and acceptance until the end.

A friend commented that Rodney had very few material possessions, no financial security, was the poorest of his friends—yet seemed to be the happiest. His last days and death only confirmed his approach to life: contented and grateful with whom he was and what he had.

Taken from an interview with Evie Chauncey, these lighthearted observations reveal Rodney's down-to-earth perspective on life and on death.

I've had terminal cancer for more than a month now and it's been one of the best times of my life, the best moments of my life. You know, as a meditator, you wonder what it will be like to die. You say to yourself, "I'm not afraid of death." However, truthfully, if someone asks you, you can't really know until you face it. But when they told me I had cancer, it was like telling me, "Oh, do you want some ice cream?" There was no negative reaction at all—nothing, not one bit of anxiety, not one bit of fear, not one bit of depression. Actually, a smile came on my face. Once they tell you you're terminal, now you're getting somewhere.

About five weeks ago I knew for the first time that it wasn't just a tumor, that it was malignant, right? Previously I hadn't really known how bad it was. I'm lying in the hallway of the hospital and I'm thinking, "I'm still not sure if I'm terminal or not." And I'm thinking, "How many times in previous lives have I lain somewhere waiting for death?" It brought a big smile to my face. I looked around and saw all these people on stretchers, and I felt so much compassion for them. I didn't want them to see me smiling at them because I didn't want to upset them. I just felt such a big smile: "Wow, this is one more life."

I got out of the hospital and a few days later went with my daughter and my friend Jerry to the G.I. guy (gastro-intestinal specialist). I walked in and we shook hands, but he seemed a little perturbed. He started off by declaring, "It's too late, it's too late." "Too late?" I asked. "Too late for what?" He said, "It's too late. I can't even do chemotherapy on you. Your cancer has spread all over the place."

"It's okay," I replied. "Then maybe I should buy a new pair of shoes to wear into the next life." The doc stood staring at me, not comprehending. I said again, "It's really okay." And I realized, hey, I'm not having any reaction. In fact, the only thing that's freaking me out is that this doctor is freaking out. He said, "You're a tough guy." "Me? Tough? What am I tough about?" After we left the office Jerry suggested he was just trying to figure me out—Why is he not reacting? Next life?—because usually everyone reacts. But actually there was no fear, no upset, no depression.

For the last several weeks, I've been getting only accolades. People come and say, "Rodney, you're amazing." Now I know what the word "amazing" is: It's Rodney. (He laughs) I'm watching this to make sure that I'm not getting into a big ego trip about it, because you really don't want your final journey to be an ego trip. (Laughs again.) Another impurity, right?

Most of the time I'm content. I've gained a lot more tolerance for people who might be difficult to deal with. If I'm talking to someone and I find he's getting upset or agitated or something, I just change the subject. He won't even notice. You know, I don't have time for anger.

There's such a lot of *mettā* from everyone—their body language, the way they look into my eyes, the way they talk to me, the way they touch me—everything they do tells me it's very different than it was before. It's on a much softer, much gentler level. People who send me e-mails and call me—I can feel it in the air, the *mettā*.

Sometimes I sit quietly and I can feel my whole body dissipating, the pain getting quiet and my mind being quiet. The pain can be pretty intense sometimes, but pain is pain—it all depends on your state of mind in the moment. You can have a little bit of pain and it seems really intense, especially if there's a lot of negativity around. Or you can have a great deal of pain, but because the positive vibrations are so strong you don't feel it.

Though I don't feel sick, my body feels like it's breaking down. But my mental state is not. I feel the vibrations here in the hospital have really gotten a lot stronger, especially because people have been coming to visit and to meditate so much. There have been times, like at 11 at night, when I'm just sitting here and my whole being goes quiet. No pain. No suffering. My mind is quiet. My body is quiet. Everything is just so quiet. Wow! People are sending me *mettā*. I've become quite in tune with that now since I've been sick. *Mettā* works!

When I was in the bush tree-planting, or anywhere, and I'd see birds or other animals, or dogs, or even a fly in the toilet and I'd put my hand in to get it out, I always wished them to be happy and to have a better birth in their next life: "Too bad you're like this now. May the rest of your life be happy and your next life be better. May you be peaceful and happy."

My son asked me, "How's your mental state, Dad?"—not how is your physical state? How is your *mental* state?—which is really great. He's been here when Dhamma friends have been visiting, and they've been talking. It's taken a little while, but now he's really getting to understand that it's the mental state that's most important.

He's realizing how good it's been during this time we've had together, rather than being sad that someone is leaving. He told me, "Dad, you know, maybe years down the road I might get myself into a situation and I will think, 'Now, how would Dad deal with this?'" So, to me, that was very good. Now he can see that the Vipassana practice is the most important thing.

He once inquired, "Dad, if someone was killing me, would you kill him?" I answered, "No, if you die in that situation, that's okay. My commitment is not to destroy life. I would do everything in my power to protect you, but I would not cross the line of killing or stealing or lying or anything against my Dhamma practice, because that's even worse than you getting killed. Even if you are killed, it's just one life, and I'm not going to take that step backwards."

Reading things by Sayagyi U Ba Khin about death—it's very encouraging. It's encouraging because he talks about how important it is to keep your *sīla*, and give *dāna*, which helps you into the celestial planes. On top of that, you have your meditation and you have your equanimity, and that's like being in a car carrying you forward in high gear, speeding ahead. You're driving the car, going through all this Dhamma stuff, and all this *mettā* is racing toward you all the time. And you have a big smile on your face.

In the past, I remember telling people, "I'm not afraid of death." But I really didn't know. You can't really know how it's going to be. Now, when I see it coming, it's like, "Wow! This *is* how I thought it would be." I wasn't sure, but Dhamma gives you so much strength.

The nurses say that the early part of the illness is the hardest. Towards the end, near death, we come to accept it. But I've accepted it right from the beginning. I haven't seen any change in my mind in all the time I've been going through this. I watch it to be sure, to see if there's any change, but there isn't.

So, what's happening is I'm facing death. I have no negativity at all, none at all. I have the Dhamma with me; I feel the strong vibrations of Dhamma around me. It feels good—it feels really good. I'm smiling all the way to death.

Sukha dukha apane karma ke,
avicala vishva vidhāna.
Tū terā Yamarāja hai,
tū tāraka bhagavāna.

Happiness and misery are the fruit
of your own actions.
This is an immutable, universal law.
You are your own lord of death;
you are your own savior.

—Hindi *doha*, S.N. Goenka

Questions to Goenkaji II
Preparing for Our Own Deaths

Student: Can any lessons be learned from the way the Buddha or his followers died?

Goenkaji: The Buddha died smilingly, giving Dhamma—a Vipassana lesson for everyone.

The Buddha was a teacher. He had the determination to give Dhamma until his last breath—and so he did. As he was dying someone came to see him, but his long-time attendant Ānanda stopped him, saying, "No, this is not the time." Overhearing him, the Buddha said, "No. Bring him, Ānanda. Bring him." His volition, his compassion was so great that he didn't care about his own pain at the time of death. He knew he had to give Dhamma to this person who otherwise might miss it. Compassion is an important quality to develop for those who are teaching.

I would like to know where we should place our attention a few hours before dying, and then where at the moment of death?

You want to be aware of sensations and *anicca* all the time. By the practice of Vipassana you learn the art of living, and you learn the art of dying. If you have been practicing Vipassana regularly, then at the time of death you will automatically become fully aware of your sensations and *anicca*, and die very peacefully. You cannot die unconscious, crying, or in fear; you pass away smiling and observing sensations. So not only is this life secured, the next life is also secured

Some people recommend that, before dying, we recollect our previous good deeds, merits like *dāna* and *sīla*, that we have accumulated. Since we are still far away from *nibbāna*, perhaps this might lead us toward a *devā loka*, a heavenly plane. Should we try to go to a heavenly plane?

For people who have never practiced Vipassana, never practiced *anicca*, this is a proper thing for them to do—to remember their good deeds, which will take them to higher *lokas* or fields of existence. But if you practice Vipassana and *anicca*, you should work with *anicca* and you will also go to a heavenly *loka* if you are not yet ready for *nibbāna*. More time might still be needed before you reach *nibbāna*, so you will go to a heavenly *loka* where you will be able to continue your practice on your own without a teacher. Because you die with a mind observing *anicca*, you'll be born with a mind observing *anicca*, and you will continue to practice Vipassana.

Many people who come to the courses say, "Since childhood I have felt these sensations; I didn't know what they were." It is because that person has been practicing in the past. So this practice will go with you.

If negative thoughts are arising and we are meditating equanimously, and death comes at that moment, what *loka* will we go to?

Even while negative thoughts are arising, at the moment of death sensations will arise immediately and automatically, and if you are practicing Vipassana you will be observing them. After death you will not go to lower fields of existence, because in the lower fields you cannot practice Vipassana with awareness of *anicca*.

You need not worry. Only if you stop practicing Vipassana will there be a need for worry. If you keep practicing regularly morning and evening, then automatically at the time of death sensations will arise—there is no doubt about that. No one practicing Vipassana needs to fear death—you will be promoted!

If you practice Vipassana, death will certainly occur in a positive way.

How can we know whether there is a past life, or life after death, without personal experience?

It is not necessary to believe in a past or future life for Vipassana to help you. Surely you must believe in this present life. Many people come to courses not believing in past or future lives—it doesn't matter. Give all importance to the reality of this moment: At this moment you are dying—every moment you are dying, every moment taking new birth. Observe that, feel that, understand that. Also understand how you react to this changing flow, and thereby harm yourself. When you stop reacting, the present becomes better and better. If there is a future life, certainly you will benefit there as well. If there is no future life, why worry? You have done your best to improve your present life. The future is nothing but the product of the present. If the present is alright, the future will be alright.

Sabbadānaṃ dhammadānaṃ jināti;
sabbarasaṃ dhammaraso jināti;
sabbaratiṃ dhammarati jināti;
taṇhakkhayo sabbadukkhaṃ jināti.

The gift of Dhamma triumphs over all other gifts;
the taste of Dhamma triumphs over all other tastes;
the happiness of Dhamma triumphs over all other pleasures;
the eradication of craving triumphs over all suffering.

—*Dhammapada* 24.354

Do not waste the time you have left. This is the time for you to strive with energy and steadfastness. You can be sure that you will die, but you can't be sure how much longer you have to live.

—Venerable Webu Sayadaw

Ratilal Mehta
1901–1987

A Life and Death in Dhamma

This story appeared in the September 1988 Vipassana Newsletter.

The Vipassana International Meditation Centre, Dhamma Khetta, near Hyderabad, was the first center to open in India. Goenkaji inaugurated it in September 1976 by planting a sapling from the sacred Bodhi Tree in Bodh Gaya and by conducting his 124th course there, attended by 122 students.

From its inception and for many years thereafter, the driving force behind the center was Mr. Ratilal Mehta, a highly successful businessman and devout member of the Jain community. His wife's untimely death in an accident brought home to him the reality of suffering and, like so many before him, Mr. Mehta began seeking a way to deal with his anguish.

An article on Dhamma Khetta in the *Vipassana Journal* recounts how Mr. Mehta, who had been searching earnestly in many spiritual traditions, overheard a conversation between a Jain monk and a professor of Jainism. The two were discussing different types of meditation, and commented upon the unique experiences of meditators who had undertaken Vipassana courses. The conversation inspired Mr. Mehta to join the next course conducted by Goenkaji.

In the practice of Vipassana he found what he had been looking for. With characteristic zeal Mr. Mehta immersed himself in the practice, taking six more courses one after the other. But this was not all. He was eager too to help others find the Dhamma that had proved so beneficial to him. He organized courses in his home, and used his influence to bring people to learn Vipassana, among them all the members of his family.

The land on which Dhamma Khetta now stands was donated by the Mehta family and Mr. Mehta personally supervised most of the construction. Although his comfortable home stood nearby, he insisted on staying for long periods at the center, living as simply as possible and devoting all his time to his own practice and to serving others.

This great devotion to the Dhamma did not, however, diminish Mr. Mehta's reverence for the tradition in which he had been raised. He continued to perform the duties of a pious Jain, and to honor and serve Jain monks and nuns. He did this recognizing that the essence of Jain teaching is the conquest of craving, aversion, and ignorance, and that Vipassana is the way to achieve this goal. He understood the universal nature of pure Dhamma, which transcends all differences of sect or philosophy.

In later years Mr. Mehta's health deteriorated as cancer spread throughout his body, causing considerable pain. In his eighties he had to undergo major surgery. The operation slowed him physically but could not restrain his urge to practice and share the Dhamma. Despite the pain and physical deterioration, he continued to oversee personally the construction at Dhamma Khetta. Having barely recovered from his operation, he joined a long course at Dhamma Giri, eager to use in the best way whatever time remained to him.

It has been a year since Mr. Mehta passed away. His death was a notable and inspiring occasion. He knew that he was dying and suffered a great deal of pain, but did not complain. He wanted to be meditating when the end was near. Members of his family and friends were present. He requested to be bathed. Returned to bed, Mr. Mehta asked to be turned towards the east and helped into a sitting position. Those in the room were meditating and a tape of Goenkaji chanting was playing. The chanting tape ended with the *bhāvatu sabba maṅgalaṃ* blessings and the response of *sādhu*, s*ādhu*, *sādhu*. Mr. Mehta's body remained upright. The doctor checked his pulse and said, "He's gone," which surprised everyone since his head had not dropped, nor had his body collapsed.

When the news of Mr. Mehta's passing reached Goenkaji, he was in California on a day between courses. Those serving the courses attended the morning group sitting as usual, with Goenkaji and Mataji present. At the end of the sitting, Goenkaji announced to the students: "I have wonderful news." It was uncommon for Goenkaji to make such an announcement, and the students were even more surprised to learn of the marvelous way in which Mr. Mehta had died.

It is rare in the West for death to be viewed in a very positive way. And yet it is truly moving to hear of the ideal passing of a devoted meditator. At the moment of death, despite his great physical discomfort, Mr. Mehta's mind was filled with awareness and equanimity, humility and love. Those present when he died, and those who heard about it later, felt fortunate to share this inspiring event.

Fellow meditators who knew Mr. Mehta recall his sprightly personality, great determination, energy, and enthusiasm. Today Dhamma Khetta, which has grown to a facility accommodating 350 students, stands as a memorial to his devoted service, a service that continues to bear fruit.

The yardstick to measure one's progress on the path of Vipassana is not the type of sensation one experiences. The yardstick is the degree to which one has succeeded in ripening one's awareness and equanimity. If a student bears this nature of the technique in mind, he or she is in no danger of going astray in the practice and will certainly keep progressing toward the goal.

—S.N. Goenka

May I be calm and serene, unruffled and peaceful.
May I develop a balanced mind.
May I observe with perfect equanimity
whatever physical sensation arises on my body.

—S.N. Goenka

Equanimity in the Face of Terminal Illness

The following article first appeared in the September 1990 Vipassana Newsletter.

About 10 years ago my wife Parvathamma was diagnosed with motor neuron disease, a rare, so far incurable, condition. She experienced a gradual wasting of the muscles of her arms, legs, and neck, and required assistance with even normal activities. Treatments by allopathic, homeopathic, ayurvedic, and naturopathic doctors produced no result. Her helplessness caused her tension and frustration. She became gloomy and wept frequently.

It was heart-rending, but everyone in the family took care that she was not put to any discomfort and that there was never any opportunity for her to feel neglected. All our efforts went toward keeping her spirits up, but she would, nevertheless, break down whenever a friend or relative called on her.

It was at this stage, about four years into the illness, that my wife attended a Vipassana course in Jaipur under the guidance of Goenkaji. She found the first day exceedingly trying, but with loving meditators around her she endured the hardship with a smile. On the fourth day, Vipassana day, she was a changed person. She experienced a flow of subtle sensations throughout her body. She was beaming with joy and felt she was even physically gaining strength. Her retreat proved to be a most beneficial 10-day sojourn.

During the following months she practiced her meditation regularly in spite of her deteriorating physical condition. Unfortunately, due to work, I had to be away in Ajmer, but whenever I returned to Jaipur I would join her in meditation. Tapes of Goenkaji's chanting and visits by local meditators inspired and supported her.

After only one Vipassana course, her nature began to change significantly. Joy emanated from her. People who came to console her went away in peace. She never complained about her illness, nor did she express regret about her miserable condition. She made frequent loving and compassionate inquiries about the welfare of visitors and their family members, wishing them happiness and joy.

The disease progressed quickly. She experienced a rapid weakening of her muscles and was administered a glucose drip and oxygen. Although experiencing extreme pain, she still retained full control of her faculties. Her body below the neck was a pitiful heap of bones and shrunken muscles, but Parvathamma's face beamed with a radiant smile. And she continued to meditate.

Two days before the end she ardently requested family members to pardon her for any harsh words she might have spoken while they had been attending her, and expressed her feelings of good fortune at having had such a kind and tolerant family.

The disease had by now spread to the muscles of her heart and lungs, and she was unable to sleep because she would be overcome by coughing if moved from a sitting position. She passed the next night comparatively peacefully asleep in her wheelchair. Whenever she awoke she requested those sitting by her side to take rest, and inquired whether others in the family were sleeping.

At 7:15 am she drank some milk which was followed by a bout of coughing, something she always dreaded. Feeling suffocated, she asked that I send for the doctor who arrived within 15 minutes. As he reached our doorstep her last breath exited with a little cough. On that morning of January 15, 1985, she passed away peacefully with a clear mind, bestowing compassionate glances on those around her.

We have learned from Goenkaji that our practice is also a preparation for dying; our family's experience is a testimony to this truth. Because of her equanimity in the midst of severe suffering, my wife was in control of her faculties throughout. She was a great inspiration to everyone, and those of us who are meditators have therefore applied Dhamma more seriously. Determined effort and regular practice have helped us weather the shock of the loss of this loving being. We regularly send her *mettā* with wishes for her freedom from all suffering.

—Mr. S. Adaviappa

The Flood of Tears

Incalculable is the beginning, brethren, of this faring on. The earliest point is not revealed of the running on, faring on, of beings cloaked in ignorance, tied to craving.

As to that, what think ye, brethren? Which is greater: the flood of tears shed by you crying and weeping as ye fare on, run on this long while, united as ye have been with the undesirable, sundered as ye have been from the desirable—or the waters in the four seas?

As we allow, lord, that we have been taught by the Exalted One, it is this that is greater: the flood of tears shed by us crying and weeping as we fare on, run on this long while, united as we have been with the undesirable, separated as we have been from the desirable—not the waters in the four seas.

Well said! Well said, brethren! Well do ye allow that so has the doctrine been taught by me. Truly the flood of tears is greater…

For many a long day, brethren, have ye experienced the death of mother, of son, of daughter, have ye experienced the ruin of kinsfolk, of wealth, the calamity of disease. Greater is the flood of tears shed by you crying and weeping over one and all of these, as ye fare on, run on this many a long day, united with the undesirable, sundered from the desirable, than are the waters in the four seas.

Why is that? Incalculable is the beginning, brethren, of this faring on. The earliest point is not revealed of the running on, the faring on of beings cloaked in ignorance, tied to craving. Thus far is enough, brethren, for you to be repelled by all the things of this world, enough to lose all passion for them, enough to be delivered therefrom.

—*Assu Sutta, Saṃyutta Nikāya* 2.126,
C.A.F. Rhys Davids, translator

The Death of Our Children

It doesn't matter how old one's children are, losing a child to death is incomprehensible suffering. So great is the grief that in many cases parents are no longer able to remain a source of strength for each other, and a marriage founders.

Grief is a very deep and painful *saṅkhāra*, but our meditation can help us cope with its intensity. Through our daily practice, both our understanding of impermanence and our development of equanimity towards it become our refuge, a sheltered place where we can regain our balance and strength to carry on.

Our practice has the potential to heal our emotions and balance our mind. On the path of equanimous acceptance, there is eventual deliverance from our suffering.

An Invaluable Gift

After her son died unexpectedly, a mother wrote to Goenkaji expressing her gratitude for the extraordinary gift of Dhamma.

I would like to tell you about the miracle of this practice which came to help me during the most devastating event of my entire life.

I am a widow and I had two children. One Sunday evening I received a call that my son had been killed in a car accident. He was 30 years old. He was my best friend. We had a perfect connection in Dhamma, in art, and on all the issues of life.

My daughter was visiting me when that striking news came and we were both paralyzed. At that moment the first thoughts were: "It is over. It is a drastic *anicca* and there is nothing we can do." The initial shock of the news made the mind react with tremendous pain. This immediately was manifesting in the body, and the adrenal glands released a poison and made me very weak on top of my chronic fatigue.

The first day I cried several times, but I noticed that the crying lasted only a few seconds because, I guess, the mind automatically went to the sensations, in contrast to the past when I used to cry for many hours.

But the second day, something amazing happened. Suddenly I felt a lot of peace, full acceptance of the event, and the mind did not feel like rolling in grief; it was like I had finished several days of *ānāpāna*. I did not understand what happened with me, as I had never experienced such a state of mind after stress. In fact I used to be a highly emotional person and I was asking myself, "Did I become insensitive or indifferent?"

In all these years of practice I did not really notice a clear equanimity in the ups and downs of everyday life. But it seems to me that, through correct and persistent practice, in time the equanimity accumulated silently drop by drop in the subconscious. Suddenly, after the shock, all its content rose to the conscious level and filled it up.

It is amazing! It has been two months since the event and it's still there. Of course, from time to time, a sudden memory comes striking like a knife into my solar plexus and into my chest. But because of the practice, the mind immediately remembers to go "breath in, breath out, to the palms," and in three or four breaths I am out of pain for long periods of time.

What an extraordinary tool we have! Some people seeing me in such a state of mind thought that I might be in denial or I might suppress the crying—perhaps to show what a Vipassana meditator I am—but I have analyzed myself and I did not find a trace of such thoughts.

So, Goenkaji, I would like to know from you if this is a common phenomenon of such a state of mind, which happens with meditators in some point of their life. If it is so, my experience is a real proof that the technique of Vipassana works miracles.

The proof is not for me, as I never had any doubt about it, but for those who have still some skepticism about it.

My son kept excellent *sīla* for eight years. He also had a very deep understanding of Dhamma with no trace of doubt, and was a very generous and equanimous person. I hope that all those qualities will give him the opportunity to become a human being again in this *Buddha Sāsana* so that he will be able to continue the purification of his mind.

I feel so honored and so blessed in this life to have met you as my teacher, from whom I have learned so much. I wish you a long and healthy life. I give my deepest gratitude to Gotama the Buddha, the chain of teachers, and especially to you, Goenkaji, for giving me such an invaluable gift.

With all my *mettā*,
Gabriela Ionita

John Wolford
1971–2007

Undying Gratitude

In 1989, when John Wolford was 18, his father Carl gave him the gift of Dhamma. What he learned and practiced enriched his life from then on. In 2005, in his mid-thirties, he was diagnosed with a malignant brain tumor and surgery soon followed. From the moment he first learned of his illness until November 2007, he purposefully dedicated his life to an increased engagement with Dhamma and to sharing it with a greater sense of gratitude, even finding gratitude for his illness.

The cancer eventually spread to his spine, ultimately causing his death. However, this allowed him to die consciously rather than in a coma, as is more usual with brain tumor patients.

Initially John did not experience significant mental or physical problems. The headaches and other symptoms, which are so common among people with brain tumors, set in only at the very end. He remained, for the most part, strong and energetic, and was therefore able to respond fully to his new-found sense of spiritual urgency.

Fortunately, he was able to give up his job and devote himself full-time to sitting and serving Vipassana courses, including the 10-day Burmese-English course he served with his wife Dhalie at Dhamma Toraṇa, Ontario, only three months before he died. He worked in the kitchen, but had to absent himself regularly because the oral chemotherapy he took each morning made him nauseous. Still, during this course, he managed to compile the stories and audio files that he had collected while traveling in Burma so he could create DVDs of this Dhamma material for the Burmese students on the course. He hardly rested until the lights went out at 10 pm each night. By this and countless other gestures, his thoughtfulness, generosity, and gratitude infused and inspired all who knew him.

Following are letters from John and his mother.

Dear Goenkaji,

It's difficult for me to tell you my "story" as there are so many aspects to it, and hard also to know how to express adequately the magnitude of my gratitude to you.

Many years ago my father brought me to my first Vipassana course, conducted by Arthur Nichols. I knew then that this was the most important thing in my life, but it has always been a struggle in various ways. This changed in February 2005, when I was unexpectedly diagnosed with a large, malignant brain tumor. Actually, my whole life has changed since then.

Based on that first diagnosis the doctors thought for some time that I would be dead in nine to 12 months. This was a shock, of course, but it also shook me in some very positive ways—in fact, Vipassana just "took over" and calmed me then and there. I was instantly grateful that I was dying of a brain tumor, which would give me some time to process things, rather than finding myself in front of an oncoming car and having mere moments before it ran me over.

During the next few months the doctors lengthened their prognosis from nine to 12 months to decades, and then shortened it again to seven to 10 years. I remained all the while grateful that I had time left to use the Dhamma as best I could. And I was grateful too that I had this invaluable tool given to me so long ago.

I was grateful for and to my wife, Dhalie, also a meditator. I initially thought what I was going through was mine alone, as it was I who had the tumor. But it quickly became clear that Dhalie was with me the whole way. We both became so quiet inside, so calm, and realized immediately what a huge advantage this was. We were grateful for the opportunity it presented to support the Dhamma in us, to develop the Dhamma in us, and to use the Dhamma in us. It helped us tremendously, and continues to help us help ourselves, and help each other.

I was also grateful that my mother, who had always been interested but "never had time" to take a course, was now interested in doing so. As one can imagine, the news of this tumor came harder for her than anyone else, and she was desperately looking for a way out of her misery. Fortunately she made a wonderful decision, and within weeks of my first operation my mother was sitting her first course with Dhalie and me, and with my father serving.

Up till then I was content that my wife, father, and brother had all sat and served courses, and I knew that however things turned out they would be OK at the end—but I couldn't say that for my mother. Now I was happy that she was taking a course, taking the seed of Dhamma, and that I could contribute in some way.

She has subsequently attended two more 10-day courses and a *Satipaṭṭhāna Sutta* course, and I have been fortunate to serve on all of them. She has maintained her daily practice easily, and now reads hardly anything but Dhamma books. We converse about Dhamma all the time—she soaks it up like a sponge, never protesting, "I'm saturated; I can't take any more." And I get to be a part of that.

I'm grateful that my health insurance company agreed to support me financially, and I have therefore been able to stop working. My time now is completely freed up to spend with family, friends, and the Dhamma. Dhalie, my mother, and I sit together regularly.

To you, Goenkaji, my Dhamma father, I have a huge debt, and am exceedingly grateful that I can continue repaying it by serving the Dhamma on your behalf in different ways. I am planting as many good seeds as I am able, serving to help you spread the Dhamma as far and wide as possible.

I am, as best I can, doing *your* service justice by developing Dhamma in me. I try to keep *sīla* scrupulously, giving it now the utmost attention. *Samādhi* and *paññā* are so precious, so valuable, and help me understand and strengthen my *sīla*. I have developed a much greater appreciation for your explanation of how "all the legs of the tripod support each other."

All of this can only be done with time, and again I am so grateful for whatever I have left. The cancer has been in remission, but recently we found that the tumor may have started growing again—we need to check this soon. This disease will probably shorten my life but, who knows, maybe the tumor won't grow again and I'll die of something else instead.

Whatever the case may be, I am here now, I have sensations now. I shall do my best to help myself, which, I'm so grateful to say, automatically means helping others as well.

Thank you, Goenkaji, for all your Dhamma teaching. Because of it, my father, mother, brother, wife, friends, and unknown thousands of people in the world are able to help themselves, which means they in turn will help countless others.

With so many thanks,
and with *mettā*,
John

From John's Mother:

Dear Goenkaji,

What can I say to express my gratitude for the invaluable benefits my family and I have gained through receiving the priceless gift of Dhamma? I am sending a few short stories to you, such a wonderful story-teller, to illustrate the power of Dhamma in my life.

First story

Last January, when I learned that my eldest son, John, at 34, had a large brain tumor, I was filled with shock and horror. By February he was admitted to hospital for brain surgery. In contrast to my own reactions, I could not fail to notice his courageous and unprotesting attitude. Instead, he showed compassion and caring for those of us who were so distressed by these unexpected events.

Shortly after the surgery, which lasted about five hours, I visited him in the recovery room. The first thing I asked was, "John, how are you feeling?" With his eyes closed and a small smile on his face, he replied, "Sensations are rising; sensations are passing away." Later, when I spoke with him about it, he could not remember saying those words. But he told me that, before entering the operating room, he started observing sensations in his body with the intention of maintaining that practice throughout the surgery, to whatever extent possible.

I know that a significant aspect of my agitation was my helplessness to save my son from this vicissitude. But I was learning that Dhamma could. Through the benefits of practice, my son was transforming something terrible into a tool, a precious gift to advance on the Dhamma path.

Second story

A few days after John's surgery I visited him at the hospital. I asked him about his practice of Vipassana. I wanted to know how it gave him remarkable strength in the face of this terrible disease. As he spoke of his experiences with Vipassana, he told me that for a long time he had maintained a wish that one day I would take a course and he would serve on that course.

In the past, both he and my younger son Dharma had suggested that I could benefit from attending a course. Naturally, for years I was always too busy! Suddenly, I wasn't busy any more! Not knowing if John would ever leave the hospital, I told him that the next course he went to, I would be there too. It seemed a small wish to grant and a way to offer my son support. I could never have guessed the benefits I would gain, nor that my son was again transforming his cancer into a vehicle for the gift of liberation—mine!

Third story

About a month later, I found myself in a car with John, his wife, Dhalie, and his father, Carl, all seasoned Vipassana meditators. We were traveling to Dhamma Kuñja in Washington state, where I was to take my first course. What a course that was! How I burned with rage and resentment against things I could not even name. How could I escape? How could I run away when my eldest son was sitting in the same room, a large tumor pressing on his brain?

I stayed, and somehow in the small intervals between being engulfed in my own chaotic reactions I tried to apply the technique I was learning. In the middle of the 10 days I wondered how I would tell my son that this path is not for me; by the end of the course I wondered how soon I might return to do it again! Since then I have attended two more 10-day courses and maintain a daily practice. In a week I plan to sit a *Satipaṭṭhāna Sutta* course at Dhamma Surabhi, British

Columbia. John will serve on that course. So that I can start to serve Dhamma in some way, I am being trained as an on-line worker to help register students as they apply for courses.

Sometime after that first course I told John that he had thrown me a lifeline, but that when I first grabbed hold it felt more like a live wire, with me sizzling, snapping, and popping on the other end! After returning home, I noticed my life changing for the better in many ways. Family and friends have told me they see a change for the better in me. Most important, I can share the precious moments in life knowing they must pass, and face the suffering without being totally engulfed in anxiety and fear.

I attribute all these benefits, and more, Goenkaji, to the inner transformation brought about by taking that first course! My relationship with all my family members has improved, and I am fortunate to be able to sit with John and Dhalie on a frequent basis and to enjoy Dhamma conversations with them as well. Their practice-in-action and their loving-kindness have been a constant inspiration to me.

It is a great comfort to see John making the best use of his time. Since he is free from working a regular job, he works instead to spread the Dhamma every day. The doctors now think that his tumor might be starting to grow again. But if his health permits, he will travel to India with Dhalie, and she will sit the Teacher's Self-Course at Dhamma Giri in November. John is on the waiting list to serve the same course. In January, my partner and I will fly to Burma and join them. We shall visit various Vipassana sites and, we hope, sit a course at a centre there. We have been accepted to sit a 10-day course at Dhamma Giri at the end of January before returning to Vancouver. That these things will happen remains to be seen. Nonetheless, it remains true that my life has changed for the better beyond anything I could have imagined.

I know I have a long way to go to dispel my own ignorance and to overcome habits of craving and aversion. With all the benefits, I am still far from equanimous about certain facts of life, including the fact that John has cancer and the doctors can do nothing to help him. I have turned to Dhamma as my life raft in these turbulent seas. I will continue to make my best efforts to sail onward.

As I wish to be free from craving, suffering, and misery,
May all beings be free from craving, suffering and misery!
May all beings be happy!

With respect and gratitude,
a humble student of Vipassana,
Laurie Campbell

Three years later:

Dear Virginia,

I'm happy to share the letter I wrote to Goenkaji. Sometime after I gave it to John to arrange for delivery, John asked if I'd give permission for some part to be printed in a newsletter or some such. I readily agreed at the time and would be happy if it might help anyone else. John's letter is here too, as you see.

I appreciated your sharing some stories of John as a young student. It brought a smile to my face.

I have one more story to share. When John was in hospital for the last time, at some point I became aware that he was unlikely to go home again. It was early November 2007. I remember saying to him one day that if he were to pass on my birthday, I would light a candle for him in my heart every year thereafter. In retrospect, it seemed a strange, macabre thing to say. I have no idea why I said it.

John died on November 20, my 59th birthday. I experienced his going as his last gift to me. I would have done anything to have my son outlive me—I know that through and through. But I was not in a position to make that happen, nor to decide what was for his own highest good. Nor, actually, what was for mine.

At the time, I thought his going on that particular day was an incredibly direct gift and message to me—he was free from suffering at last, and those final days and weeks were terrible for what he endured. Since then, as my birthday approaches, I reflect both on John and his amazing loving generosity of spirit, and on my own approaching, inevitable death. I know he's made my own time of letting go easier, whenever it will come. In the meantime, my understanding of *anicca* has been profoundly deepened.

From the moment John learned he had a brain tumor, through to his death, his own personal process of growth and development accelerated. It was amazing to watch his sharp edges melt away, and to witness and enjoy the loving energy he so freely shared with whomever he came in contact. Near the end, it was a privilege to watch the dissolution of his ego and the complete emergence of the essence of being: love. The vehicle for his transformation was his practice of Vipassana, there is no doubt. John took a crash course in the art of living and came through in fine form.

It was his great good fortune to receive the gift of Dhamma through his father. One can't see the miracle of John's journey exclusive of Carl's influence, and in my heart I owe Carl a huge debt of gratitude in bringing both of our sons to Dhamma. I am forever in his debt, but then, as he has pointed out to me, the ripples and the debt spread out to include all who helped *him* along the path, back and back through teachers and students, all the way to the Buddha.

It has been an amazing journey—painful, and yet rich with gifts of love and compassion. So much has come my way, including the loving-kindness of many who were touched by John and in turn magnanimously extended themselves to me.

I'm afraid, though, that I'm not at all like some of the writers who people your book. As the anniversary of John's death approaches I'm aware of the awful pain of loss, the resurfacing of barely concealed grief. However adept I may be at employing my intellect to make sense of it all, and even in times of more integrated knowing, the harsh fact of his ending still grieves me beyond speech. I am not equanimous, and the best I can do is sit with the pain, endure, and try to apply compassion to my seemingly intractable clinging. I know the grief is all to do with me, what I want, how I wish the universe to be ordered. Should I grieve that my son is free of this lifetime's suffering? That he was successful in transforming the basest of metals to gold? Should I grieve that he grew and grew in love until that was all that remained?

When I think of my children, I am amazed. They have been teachers on so many levels, and I'm in awe that somehow I have had them in my life. John has been gone almost three years now, yet in many ways he is with me still, influencing and guiding. I am a most fortunate mother.

With all the *mettā*,
Laurie

Attanā hi kataṃ pāpaṃ,
attanā saṃkilissati;
Attanā akataṃ pāpaṃ,
attanāva visujjhati.
Suddhī asuddhi paccattaṃ,
nāñño aññaṃ visodhaye.

By self alone is evil done.
By self alone is one defiled.
By self alone is evil not done.
By self alone is one purified.
Purity and impurity depend on oneself.
No one can purify another.

—*Dhammapada* 12.165

Pralayaṅkārī bādha meṅ,
tū hī terā dvīpa.
andhakāramaya rāta meṅ,
tū hī terā dīpa.

In the all-destroying deluge
you alone are your island.
In the darkest night
you alone are your lamp.

—Hindi *doha,* S.N. Goenka

Work Out Your Own Salvation

As we practice daily, morning and evening, Vipassana stays alive within us. The awareness of bodily sensations, our early warning system, alerts us to reactions that keep reinforcing our unwholesome habits. As we work to change this pattern, the need to become masters of our minds becomes crystal clear.

The process is simple, but subtle. It is easy to slip, and an uncorrected divergence can continue to widen because the path is exceedingly long. Therefore, as opportunity permits, it is good to review the correct way to practice through sitting courses and listening carefully to Goenkaji's elucidating discourses.

This article, which appeared in the spring 1997 issue of the Vipassana Newsletter, *is an abridgement of a discourse given by Goenkaji on the second day of a three-day course for experienced students. Here he carefully reviews the technique of Vipassana, explaining the practice in detail.*

At the surface, the mind plays so many games—thinking, imagining, dreaming, giving suggestions. But deep inside the mind remains a prisoner of its own habit pattern; and the habit pattern at the deepest level of the mind is to feel sensations and react. If the sensations are pleasant, the mind reacts with craving. If they are unpleasant, it reacts with aversion.

The enlightenment of the Buddha was to go to the root of the problem. Unless we work at the root level, we shall be dealing only with the intellect and only this part of the mind will be purified. As long as the roots of a tree are unhealthy, the whole tree will be sick. If the roots are healthy, then they will provide healthy sap for the entire tree. So start working with the roots—this was the enlightenment of the Buddha.

When he gave Dhamma, the path of morality, concentration and wisdom (*sīla, samādhi* and *paññā*), it was not to establish a cult, a dogma, or a belief. The Noble Eightfold Path is a practical path and those who walk on it can go to the deepest level of the mind and eradicate all their miseries.

Those who have really liberated themselves know that going to the depth of the mind—making a surgical operation of the mind—has to be done by oneself, by each individual. Someone can guide you with love and compassion; someone can help you on your journey along the path. But nobody can carry you on his shoulders, saying, "I will take you to the final goal. Just surrender to me. I will do everything."

You are responsible for your own bondage. You are responsible for making your mind impure—no one else. Only you are responsible for purifying your mind, for breaking the bonds.

Continuity of practice is the secret of success. When it is said that you should be continuously aware, it means that you must be aware with wisdom of sensations in the body, where you really experience things arising and passing away. This awareness of impermanence is what purifies your mind—the awareness of the sensations arising, passing.

Intellectualizing this truth will not help. You may understand: "Everything that arises sooner or later passes away. Anyone who takes birth sooner or later dies. This is *anicca*." You might understand this correctly but you are not experiencing it. It is your own personal experience that will help you purify your mind and liberate you from your miseries. The word for "experience" used in India at the time of the Buddha was *vedanā*, feeling by experiencing, not just by intellectualization. And this is possible only when sensations are felt in the body.

Anicca must be experienced. If you are not experiencing it, it is merely a theory, and the Buddha was not interested in theories. Even before the Buddha, and at the time of the Buddha, there were teachers who taught that the entire universe is in flux, *anicca*—this was not new. What was new from the Buddha was the *experience* of *anicca*; and when you experience it within the framework of your own body, you have started working at the deepest level of your mind.

Two things are very important for those who walk on the path. The first is breaking the barrier that divides the conscious and the unconscious mind. But even if your conscious mind can now feel those sensations that were previously felt only by the deep unconscious part of your mind, that alone will not help you.

The Buddha wanted you to take a second step: change the mind's habit of reacting at the deepest level.

Coming to the stage where you have started feeling sensations is a good first step, yet the habit pattern of reaction remains. When you feel an unpleasant sensation, if you keep reacting—"Oh, I must get rid of this"—that won't help. If you start feeling a pleasant flow of very subtle vibrations throughout the body, and you react—"Ah, wonderful! This is what I was looking for. Now I've got it!"—you have not understood Vipassana at all.

Vipassana is not a game of pleasure and pain. You have been reacting like this your entire life, for countless lifetimes. Now in the name of Vipassana you have started making this pattern stronger. Every time you feel an unpleasant sensation you react in the same way, with aversion. Every time you feel pleasant sensation you react in the same way, with craving. Vipassana has not helped you because you have not helped Vipassana.

Whenever you again make the mistake of reacting because of the old habit, see how quickly you become aware of it: "Look—an unpleasant sensation and I am reacting with aversion; a pleasant sensation and I am reacting with craving. This is not Vipassana. This will not help me."

Understand, this is what you have to do. If you are not 100 percent successful, it doesn't matter. This won't harm you as long as you keep understanding and keep trying to change the old habit pattern. If for even a few moments you have started coming out of your prison, then you are progressing.

This is what the Buddha wanted you to do: practice the Noble Eightfold Path. Practice *sīla* so that you can have the right type of *samādhi*. For those who keep breaking *sīla*, there is little hope that they will go to the deepest levels of reality. *Sīla* develops after you have some control over your mind, after you start understanding with *paññā* that breaking *sīla* is very harmful. Your *paññā* at the experiential level will help your *samādhi*. Your *samādhi* at the experiential level will help your *sīla*. Your stronger *sīla* will help your *samādhi* become strong. Your stronger *samādhi* will help your *paññā* become strong. Each of the three will help the other two, and you will keep progressing.

You must be with reality, with the truth as it is. Things keep changing. All vibrations are nothing but a flux, a flow. This realization removes the deep-rooted habit pattern of reacting to the sensations.

Whatever sensations you experience—pleasant, unpleasant or neutral—you should use them as tools. These sensations can become tools to liberate you from your misery, provided you understand the truth as it is. But these same sensations can also become tools that multiply your misery. Likes and dislikes should not cloud the issue. The reality is: sensations are arising and passing away; they are *anicca*. Pleasant, unpleasant or neutral—it makes no difference. When you start realizing the fact that even the most pleasant sensations you experience are *dukkha* (suffering), then you are coming nearer to liberation.

Understand why pleasant sensations are *dukkha*. Every time a pleasant sensation arises, you start relishing it. This habit of clinging to pleasant sensations has persisted for countless lifetimes. And it is because of this that you have aversion. Craving and aversion are two sides of the same coin. The stronger the craving, the stronger the aversion is bound to be. Sooner or later every pleasant sensation turns into an unpleasant one, and every unpleasant sensation will turn into a pleasant one—this is the law of nature. If you start craving pleasant sensations, you are inviting misery.

The Buddha's teaching helps us to disintegrate the solidified intensity that keeps us from seeing the real truth. In reality, there are mere vibrations, nothing else. At the same time, there is solidity. For example, this wall is solid. This is a truth, an apparent truth. The ultimate truth is that what you call a wall is nothing but a mass of vibrating subatomic particles. We have to integrate both truths through proper understanding.

Dhamma develops our understanding, so that we free ourselves from the habit of reacting and recognize that craving is harming us, hating is harming us. Then we are more realistic: "See, there is ultimate truth, and there is apparent truth, which is also a truth."

The process of going to the depth of the mind to liberate yourself has to be done by you alone, but you must also be prepared to work with your family, with society as a whole. The yardstick to measure whether love, compassion, and good will are truly developing is whether these qualities are being exhibited toward the people around you.

The Buddha wanted us to be liberated at the deepest level of our minds. And that is possible only when three characteristics are realized: *anicca* (impermanence), *dukkha* (suffering), and *anattā* (egolessness). When the mind starts to become free from conditioning, layer after layer becomes purified until the mind is totally unconditioned. Purity then becomes a way of life. You won't have to practice *mettā* (compassionate love) as you do now at the end of your one-hour sitting. Later, *mettā* just becomes your life. All the time you will remain suffused with love, compassion, and good will. This is the aim, the goal.

The path of liberation is the path of working at the deepest level of the mind. There is nothing wrong with giving good mental suggestions, but unless you change the blind habit of reacting at the deepest level, you are not liberated. Nobody is liberated unless the deepest level of the mind is changed, and the deepest level of the mind is constantly in contact with bodily sensations.

We have to divide, dissect, and disintegrate the entire structure to understand how mind and matter are so interrelated. If you work only with the mind and forget the body, you are not practicing the Buddha's teaching. If you work only with the body and forget the mind, again you do not properly understand the Buddha.

Anything that arises in the mind turns into matter, into a sensation in the material field. This was the Buddha's discovery. People forgot this truth, which can only be understood through proper practice. The Buddha said, "*Sabbe dhammā vedanā samosaraṇā*"—"Anything that arises in the mind starts flowing as a sensation on the body."

The Buddha used the word *āsava*, which means flow or intoxication. Suppose you have generated anger. A biochemical flow starts that generates very unpleasant sensations. Because of these unpleasant sensations, you start reacting with anger. As you generate anger, the flow becomes stronger. There are unpleasant sensations and, with them, a biochemical secretion. As you generate more anger, the flow becomes stronger.

In the same way, when passion or fear arises, a particular type of biochemical substance starts flowing in the blood. A vicious circle starts that keeps repeating itself. There is a flow, an intoxication, at the depth of the mind. Out of ignorance we get intoxicated by this particular biochemical flow. Although it makes us miserable, yet we are intoxicated; we want it again and again. So we keep on generating anger upon anger, passion upon passion, and fear upon fear. We become intoxicated by whatever impurity we generate in our minds. If we say that someone is addicted to alcohol or drugs, this is actually untrue. No one is addicted to alcohol or drugs. The truth is that one is addicted to the sensations that are produced by the alcohol or drugs.

The Buddha teaches us to observe reality. Every addiction will be undone if we observe the truth of sensations in the body with this understanding: "*Anicca, anicca.* This is impermanent." Gradually we will learn to stop reacting.

Dhamma is so simple, so scientific, so true—a law of nature applicable to everyone. Buddhist, Hindu, Muslim, Christian; American, Indian, Burmese, Russian, or Italian—it makes no difference; a human being is a human being. Dhamma is a pure science of mind, matter, and the interaction between the two. Don't allow it to become a sectarian or philosophical belief. This will be of no help.

The greatest scientist the world has produced worked to find the truth about the relationship between mind and matter. And discovering this truth, he found a way to go beyond mind and matter. He explored reality not for the sake of curiosity but to find a way to be free of suffering. For every individual there is so much misery—for every family, for every society, for every nation, for the entire world—so much misery. The Enlightened One found a way to be free of this misery.

Each individual has to come out of misery. There is no other solution. Every member of a family must come out of misery. Then the family will become happy, peaceful, and harmonious. If every member of society comes out of misery, if every member of a nation comes out of misery, if every citizen of the world comes out of misery, only then will there be world peace.

There can't be world peace just because we want world peace—"I am agitating for world peace; therefore it should occur." This doesn't happen. We can't agitate for peace. When we are agitated, we lose our own peacefulness. So, no agitation! Purify your mind; then every action you take will add peace to the universe.

Purify your mind. This is how you can help society; this is how you can stop harming others and start helping them. When you work for your own liberation, you will find that you have also started helping others to come out of their misery. One individual becomes several individuals—a slow widening of the circle. There is no magic, no miracle. Work for your own peace, and you will find that you have started making the atmosphere around you more peaceful—provided you work properly.

If there is any miracle, it is the miracle of changing the habit pattern of the mind from rolling in misery to freedom from misery. There can be no bigger miracle than this. Every step taken toward this kind of miracle is a healthy step, a helpful step. Any other apparent miracle is bondage.

May you all come out of your misery and become free of your bondage. Enjoy real peace, real harmony, real happiness.

—S.N. Goenka

Aciraṃ vatayaṃ kāyo,
pathaviṃ adhisessati;
Chuddho apetaviññāṇo,
niratthaṃva kaliṅgaraṃ.

Alas! Ere long this corporeal body
will lie flat upon the earth,
unheeded, devoid of consciousness,
like a useless log of wood.

—*Dhammapada* 3.41

Hiding from the Wisdom of *Anicca*

For centuries, humans have devised countless products in an attempt to improve the appearance of the body, disguise its odor, halt its decay, mask its physical and mental pain—all to create an illusion of beauty, happiness, and constancy. Markets flourish selling jewelry, fashionable clothing, hair dyes, makeup, anti-wrinkle creams, deodorants, perfumes, alcohol, drugs, and more.

The truth of the material body has been buried deep in the unconscious mind, and its products are the soil that covers the casket. The Buddha unearthed the truth of material form. He understood experientially its moment-to-moment decay and the overall withering that leads to death, and discovered that the truth of *anicca* within the body was the key to *nibbāna*.

We all have inklings of this truth but hide from it, because it exposes a deeply pervasive fear of loss entangled with our strong attachment to the mistaken perception of a permanent body housing an eternal "I."

Vipassana meditation brings the mind-body's true nature into view, with its incessant changing quality—*anicca*. Developing equanimity towards the reality of the mind-body is what breaks down our attachment to it and leads us to liberation.

Ambapālī's Verses

At the time of the Buddha, Ambapālī was an exquisitely beautiful and famous courtesan. She had a son who became an eminent elder in the Buddha's monastic order. One day she heard her son give a discourse on Dhamma and was inspired by its truth to renounce the world and ordain as a bhikkhunī. *Through observation of the decay of her once-beautiful body, she understood the law of impermanence to its full extent and became an* arahant.

This selection of her verses describes the changes that transform the body in old age.

My hair was black, the color of bees,
each hair ending in a curl.
Now, on account of old age,
they have become like fibers of hemp.
Not otherwise is the word
of the Speaker of Truth.

Covered with flowers, my head was fragrant
like a casket of delicate scent.
Now, on account of old age,
it smells like the fur of a dog.
Not otherwise is the word
of the Speaker of Truth.

Formerly my eyebrows were beautiful,
like crescents well painted by an artist's hand.
Now, on account of old age,
they droop down, lined by wrinkles.
Not otherwise is the word
of the Speaker of Truth.

Brilliant and beautiful like jewels,
my eyes were dark blue and long in shape.
Now, hit hard by old age,
their beauty has utterly vanished.
Not otherwise is the word
of the Speaker of Truth.

Formerly my teeth looked beautiful,
the color of plantain buds.
Now, on account of old age,
they are broken and yellow.
Not otherwise is the word
of the Speaker of Truth.

Formerly my two breasts were beautiful,
swollen, round, compact, and high.
Now they hang down and sag,
like a pair of empty water bags.
Not otherwise is the word
of the Speaker of Truth.

Formerly my body was beautiful,
like a well-polished sheet of gold.
Now it is all covered with wrinkles.
Not otherwise is the word
of the Speaker of Truth.

Formerly my feet looked beautiful,
as if made of cotton wool.
Now, because of old age,
they are cracked and wrinkled all over.
Not otherwise is the word
of the Speaker of Truth.

Such is this body, now decrepit,
the abode of a jumble of suffering.
It is nothing but an aged house
from which the plaster has fallen.
Not otherwise is the word
of the Speaker of Truth.

—*Therīgāthā* 13.252–270,
Amadeo Solé-Leris, translator

Dvipādakoyaṃ asuci,
duggandho parihārati;
Nānākuṇapaparipūro,
vissavanto tato tato.
Etādisena kāyena,
yo maññe uṇṇametave;
Paraṃ vā avajāneyya
kimaññatra adassanāti.

This two-footed dirty body,
carrying about a bad odor
and full of impurities
that pour out from different places—
with a body like this,
if one thinks highly of oneself
and looks down upon others,
to what can this be due, except ignorance?

—*Sutta Nipata* 1.207-208

Questions to Goenkaji III

Ethical Questions in the Age of Modern Medicine

Suppose, as death approaches, someone refuses food or treatment. She knows she's dying and she feels she can't bear it any more. Is that considered suicide?

Again, it depends. If she refuses food with the intention of dying prematurely, then it is wrong. But if she stops taking food or medicine, saying, "Let me die peacefully; don't disturb me," that's a different thing. It all depends on the volition. If the volition is to die quickly, it's wrong. If the volition is to die peacefully, it's totally different.

Doctors in the West treat patients as long as they can. However, when they decide that nothing more can be done medically, there is a system by which patients are allowed to return home and are provided nursing care so they can die peacefully in familiar surroundings. Usually, all that's given for treatment is palliative medication, and care and comfort.

Wonderful! Very good! This is the humane way. If he is dying and there is no further treatment, it is better to take him home to a good atmosphere. Create a Dhamma atmosphere. Let him die peacefully, in comfort. Good.

Na antalikkhe na samuddamajjhe,
na pabbatānaṃ vivaraṃ pavissa;
Na vijjatī so jagatippadeso,
yatthaṭṭhitaṃ nappasaheyya maccu.

Not in the sky, not in the middle of the ocean,
not even in the cave of a mountain
should one seek refuge;
for there exists no place in the world
where one will not be overpowered by death.

—*Dhammapada* 9.128

Terrell Jones
1942–2002

Facing Death Head-on

In 2002, Terrell Jones died from cancer at his home in Copper Hill, Virginia. Eight years earlier he had discovered Vipassana, and soon afterwards his wife Diane also attended a course. Together they became serious meditators, sitting and serving as much as possible.

Even the knowledge of his imminent death could not deter them from serving. In the weeks before his death, he and Diane were fully occupied as registrars for a nearby non-center course.

Two weeks before he died, Diane drove Terrell 12 hours north to the Vipassana Meditation Center, Dhamma Dharā, in Massachusetts, where Goenkaji and his wife Mataji were visiting. They wished to pay respects to them and express their gratitude for the gift of Vipassana. Throughout their visit Terrell was an inspiration to all: no fear, no regrets—just joy and gratitude.

Terrell had only 10 weeks to come to terms not only with terminal cancer, but with losing his love of 30 years. He had, as well, to face the fact that he would not be present to help and comfort her.

As she watched his body withering, Diane had the same 10 weeks to learn to cope with the death of her husband of 30 years. In her mind, she faced his death each day.

Terrell and Diane had always wanted to find a way to diminish their mutual attachment, so that whoever survived the other would suffer less intense grief at the loss. They both knew that Vipassana was the way.

They meditated together every day, sometimes for many hours. They maintained their awareness of sensations in the sadness of their prolonged parting and, as equanimously as possible, watched their grief and fear. Terrell's fervent wish, near the end, was to have a peaceful mind, full of equanimity, with a strong awareness of sensations at the moment of death—a wish that was fulfilled.

While in Massachusetts, Terrell and Diane gladly agreed to be interviewed, and to share their thoughts and feelings about their lives and his impending death.

Terrell: Well, you know I have cancer with, the doctors say, only a very slim chance of beating it. But that's just a game with numbers. The way that Diane and I are dealing with it is, actually—we're happy. Crazy as it sounds, we've found the cancer to be a gift because it has shown us so much that we were previously unaware of in our day-to-day lives. Every day we recognize more people and things to be grateful for. In the past we just, I suppose, took them for granted—especially our friends who love us, whom we were too little aware of. We don't have—or at least, we might not have—that much time left, so we don't take things for granted any more. We always feel so fortunate for what we have.

Virginia: Are you afraid?

No, I'm not afraid. What's there to be afraid of? I might die in the next 30 days, I don't know. But I might not die for 30 years. Even if I have another 30 years, I'm not going to be any more ready to die then than I am now. I'm still going to have to go through exactly what I'm going through now. At this moment I have a 50-50 chance of getting through it. I'm either going to come through it alive, or come through it dead: 50-50.

Death is absolutely inevitable. Every single one of us will die sometime. Those who haven't been given their sentence by the medical profession, they're out there. But they're busy; they aren't sitting around thinking every minute about death. Whereas I don't have a lot of other things to think about, so perhaps my focus is a bit sharper than theirs.

Tell me about your discovery of Vipassana.

I was chatting with a friend one night and mentioned that I was having trouble with people; I just couldn't talk with anybody. He said, "You know, I took this course once and spent 10 days in Noble Silence," and I wanted to go for that alone. Amazingly, even though he hadn't kept up his practice, he had with him those two little information booklets that are sent to people who are curious, who want to know about courses. He still had them in a suitcase. I read them and immediately wanted to go.

But I wouldn't have gone if it hadn't been on a donation basis. Because I had been in and out of various groups, I was very skeptical. Once I got into a group and started looking a little deeper, I always found something commercial in it for somebody's financial gain. But offering Vipassana free of charge showed me this organization's volition was different. I was here at the center within six weeks of having read those two brochures.

When I came out of that 10-day course my mind began to circle back to all the problems I had back home and, incredibly, they weren't there. The reactions I would have had to certain thoughts about family or friends were all gone. I was filled with awareness of what I had, of how grateful I should have been for the people in my life who put up with my behavior as long as they had. I couldn't wait to get on the phone with Diane to tell her how much I loved her and to beg her to give me another chance. Not long after she too went to a course and from that time on, you know, we've practiced very deeply, several times a year, many courses. Our understanding has deepened. The solution to all our different problems has come down to: purify, purify, purify.

Since we had always been so much in love with each other, our goal then became gaining enough wisdom in Vipassana so that when one of us was dying we would be able to go through it without totally falling apart. And we are extremely fortunate that we attained that goal. We didn't know it, you know. We didn't know that we had attained the goal until it happened. We had no idea how we would react to one of us facing death, no idea at all. When it happened, we discovered that an entirely new understanding of what death is had taken place on a very deep level within us. Beneath the rational mind, on the unconscious level, something had gone; it had been purified by the practice of Vipassana.

In this experience we're having with death right now, I can't exactly say ... I can't really say in words what isn't there any more. Whatever it was that used to make me react with fear to the thought of dying is no longer there. I can't explain it, except that somehow all the years of meditation have eliminated that, have cut that problem off at the root. It's wonderful.

Diane, how do *you* deal with yourself and your sensations when you see Terrell in great pain? How do you cope with not being able to relieve it? Do you help in some other way, psychologically?

Diane: Often, with this cancer, Terrell's experiencing a great deal of discomfort. Loving him as I do, I always want to be able to help him with that. But there are many times when I'm unable to do so. I try to make his position more comfortable and give him things like his medication to try to help him, but often it doesn't work. There are moments when I feel like, "Gee, what else can I do?"

I want to help but, in fact, I can't really do that much physically. That's where meditation is helpful. I'll say, "Terrell, let's focus on our breath; let's focus on our sensations." He'll focus on his pain and I'll focus on mine.

My pain is the pain of feeling helpless, and yet that's always changing, that's *anicca*. It changes from moment to moment. I have these feelings sometimes of wanting to help and being unable to, and that's when my strength comes. It comes from within, from years of practicing and becoming aware of what's happening in the moment and being equanimous with that—having a balanced mind, and being aware of *anicca*.

So when those times come, I focus on my breath because that's where what Goenkaji calls "little volcanoes" come up. I can feel them coming, and as they do I focus on my breath; I focus on the sensations. Sometimes I might even cry. When the tears come, I feel them burning my face. I focus on that; I focus on the tears falling. I focus on the lump in my throat. As I feel sensations throughout my body, it eases the discomfort. I can help him more by his seeing that it works and, when he sees that, he's more focused. It's a partnership. It works both ways. When he sees me in discomfort, he does the same for me.

Many people might now consider your position to be the more difficult one, since you will be the one left behind.

I know, I hear that all the time. "You're the caregiver, and the one who's left behind is going to have it more difficult." But, like we said before, our practice has given us strength and understanding of *anicca*—change, change, change. When he passes I'll have the strength of my practice, the strength of Vipassana, and *mettā*, love. All the people who have supported us through the years, and the practice, give me strength. I am so grateful for Vipassana coming into my life through him. We've grown, we've grown with an understanding that's far beyond words. I can't express it.

We've meditated together every day since the day we started. We've never wavered. It's always been an important part of our lives. As we've become older, giving service has also become very important. In the last few years, we decided that we would spend the rest of our lives just serving and sitting. That would not only help spread the Dhamma, but it would help us strengthen our practice. Our day-to-day practice and our commitment are strong.

Terrell, could you talk about service?

Terrell: Giving service is as incredible as sitting a Vipassana course. Service is another entire course in itself. I did my first 20-day service last year. I fell in love with serving long courses. You're there serving every day. You're doing it because you're grateful for what's been given to you, and you want to give it to others. That feeling of wanting to serve others is a beautiful feeling—uplifting and so satisfying. You know that you're giving the gift of your time so that others can practice Vipassana, but the gift that servers receive is just as valuable, if not more so. It's wonderful to look out across a sea of meditators and know that you have to be a part of it for it to take place. Every person there, from the teacher to the one cleaning the toilets, is necessary—they just have different functions. Some take more training than others but, without the servers, the course couldn't happen at all.

How do you find a balance between fighting for your life and achieving a calm acceptance of the medical verdict?

I find myself in the circumstance of having terminal cancer. Strange words. I have never really thought of myself as having terminal cancer. In the medical literature, and in all the alternative therapies I've read about, if I find something that has worked, seems to have worked, has been highly touted as helping, or has helped before, I try it. But I'm not attached, because I'm not afraid to die.

I'm going to die now, 10 years from now, 20 years from now, 30 years from now—I *am* going to die. There's no getting around the fact that I'm going to die. Therefore I'm not desperate that something has to work. It doesn't have to work now. If it works, great: Diane and I have much more time to sit and serve. If it doesn't work, great: we've had this fabulous time together. We came to the Dhamma together. All these wonderful things have happened to us. We're filled with gratitude. We're going to be happy no matter what.

A month after Terrell's death, Diane returned to Massachusetts to meditate. She recounted her memories of his passing and the time leading up to it.

Diane: On the morning of his death, we got up and meditated. Later, while talking to a friend on the phone I heard Terrell say, "Diane, you need to come here now." "Okay, I replied." and hung up. When I got in there he told me, "It's time." Again, I said, "Okay."

We talked a little and he asked, "Make sure I'm doing it right. Am I doing it right, honey?" I reassured him, "Yes, you are doing it right."

He was so aware, he was starting to glow. His skin color changed; he just glowed! My friend who was with me looked at him and confirmed, "He's glowing." He was so filled with love, so filled with compassion, and the Dhamma was just ... you could see, he was aglow. He was totally in it.

He said to me, "It's okay, honey. You're going to be fine." He had no fear; he was aware of everything around him. He looked at me. "Honey, I'm losing my eyesight; it's going now," and he puckered up for me to kiss him. I kissed him.

At that moment, that's all I could do—to thank him for giving me this great gift of Dhamma. It wasn't really hard to let go because the Dhamma was fully there; it just was. I felt no holding on.

Before he died, he began to chant. He wasn't gasping for breath; it was a very calm and beautiful breath filled with love, filled with compassion for the whole world. I wasn't "me," there was no "I," no "me," no "mine." That moment was so pure; I had totally surrendered to the Dhamma.

We had been very attached to each other and knew it wasn't good. We had hoped that Vipassana would show us the way to get past it. I often wondered if it would really work when the final moment came—and it did. I was losing the love of my life, my best friend, my mentor. I let him go; I didn't cling or try to hold on to him. I didn't even have to think about it; it simply happened that way. It was not only a joy, it was an honor to be with him and experience this with him, to help him through those last moments. I was filled with joy. It's hard to explain.

As he took his last breath, an energy went through me that I can't really explain. It just shot through me, a good energy. It was comforting, and I knew at that moment that he had gone—from life to death.

It was then that something became clear to me. I finally understood—nine years I had been meditating, being aware of sensations and being equanimous with the understanding of *anicca*—it was so clear to me, crystal clear: this was *anicca*. This was it.

My heart was wide open. I was not Diane. I was totally in the present moment with full understanding of *anicca*, the impermanence of it all. I was totally unattached to everything, and I was so filled with joy that he was able to give me this gift of the understanding of this moment. I shall have that with me forever and, I hope, be able to share it with other people.

After Terrell took his last breath in this life, there were tears but no grief—only overwhelming joy. It is hard to explain that, because people feel that, when you have just lost the love of your life, you should be totally beside yourself. But I was filled with *mettā*.

A few hours after he died, people came to take his body to the funeral home. I sat in the rocking chair in the living room by myself. I looked around at all his treasures and realized the only treasure he took with him was his Dhamma.

For a while, I couldn't make decisions. I'd go to do something and just stand there as if I were waiting for him. We always made decisions together, even little ones. This closeness is what people miss when they've been with someone for a long time. There's an emptiness that is very hard to deal with.

Since his death, there have been tears and moments of grief. I miss him but, because I have this practice, I can get on my cushion. I sit there and focus on my breath—even if tears are wet on my cheeks—observing loneliness, sadness, emptiness, the pain in my heart—feeling sorry for myself. I just observe it and let it do its thing.

Jarā vyādhi se mauta se,
lade akelā eka.
Koī sātha na de sake,
parijana svajana aneka.

Old age, sickness, death,
we face these all alone.
No one can share them with us,
though many be near and dear.

—Hindi *doha,* S.N. Goenka

S.N. Goenka
1924–2013

70 Years Are Over

What follows is the translation of an article by Goenkaji, originally published in the February 1994 issue of the Hindi Vipaśhyana Patrika.

My life has seen 70 autumns. Who knows how many more are left? How can the ones that remain be best used? May this awareness be maintained.

On this occasion some beneficial words of the Buddha come to mind. They were spoken in Sāvatthī, in Anāthapiṇḍika's Jetavanarāma. At nighttime a *devaputta* came to meet the Buddha. He expressed his thoughts to the Buddha in the form of a *gāthā* of four lines:

Accenti kālā, tarayanti rattiyo
Vayoguṇā anupubbaṃ jahanti
Etaṃ bhayaṃ maraṇe pekkhamāno
Puññāni kayirātha sukhāvahāni

Time is passing, nights are passing.
Life is gradually coming to an end.
Observing the fear of (approaching) death
Perform meritorious deeds that yield pleasant fruits.

Someone rightly said, "Morning comes, evening comes; in the same way the end of life comes." Therefore do not let this priceless human life end in vain. Perform meritorious deeds that yield pleasant fruit, even if only out of fear of approaching death. If we perform wholesome deeds, they will result in happiness; if we perform unwholesome deeds, they will result in suffering for us—this is an unbreakable law of nature. Therefore, to avoid suffering and enjoy happiness, it is better to do wholesome deeds rather than unwholesome deeds.

We do not know how long we have been crushed under the ever-changing wheel of existence—neither the extent of worldly happiness and suffering in this life, nor for how long this wheel of worldly happiness and suffering will continue in future.

The Buddha discovered a simple and direct path to full liberation from this wheel of existence and made it easily accessible to all. He taught people the liberation-endowing technique of Vipassana, by the practice of which they can free themselves from the wheel of existence and attain the eternal, unchanging, *nibbānaṃ paramaṃ sukhaṃ*—ultimate happiness, the ultimate peace of *nibbāna*—infinitely superior to all worldly pleasures.

But this liberation is only possible when the habit of heedlessly running after the enjoyment of worldly pleasures is broken. And this is what Vipassana enables us to do: break the habit of multiplication of the *saṅkhāras* of craving and aversion that lie in the depths of the subconscious mind. It digs out the *saṅkhāras* of craving for pleasure and aversion toward suffering. It eradicates the longstanding habit of blind reaction.

As long as craving for sensual pleasures remains, aversion will continue to arise toward worldly suffering, and because of craving and aversion the wheel of existence will continue to roll. Only when the wheel of existence breaks can ultimate peace, which is supramundane—beyond worlds, beyond the round of existence, beyond the field of the senses—be attained. For this purpose the Buddha taught the indispensable technique of Vipassana.

Therefore, upon hearing the *gāthā*, the Buddha changed the fourth line:

Lokāmisaṃ pajahe santipekkho

One who hopes for ultimate peace
should give up the desire for worldly happiness.

Only by the ardent practice of Vipassana can one eradicate worldly desires. While practicing Vipassana, a meditator should maintain awareness of his impending death, but there should not be a trace of fear. Whenever death comes, one should be constantly prepared for it with a tranquil mind.

On his birthday, a Vipassana meditator should certainly consider the past. He should make a firm resolution not to repeat mistakes previously committed, and to continue to perform wholesome deeds for the rest of his life. The most important wholesome deed of all is the practice of the liberating technique of Vipassana. Diligently practice it; do not neglect it. Do not postpone today's practice to tomorrow. Let these words of the Buddha constantly echo in your ears like a warning:

Ajjeva kiccamātappaṃ
Kojaññā maraṇaṃ suve

Perform the work of meditation today itself.
(Do not postpone it.)
Who knows, death might come tomorrow.

One does not invite death, but when it comes there is no need to be afraid of it. Let us be prepared every moment.

From time to time we should practice *maraṇānusati* (awareness of death). By my own experience I have seen that this is very beneficial. While practicing, one should examine one's mind: "If I die tomorrow morning, what will be the nature of my last mind-moment of this life? Will any clinging remain, even to complete some Dhamma mission?"

Whenever a *saṅkhāra* of some intense emotion arises in the mind, we should immediately practice *maraṇānusati* and understand, "If I die in the very next moment, in what fearful direction will this emotion deflect the stream of becoming?" As soon as this awareness arises, it is easy to be free of that emotion.

There is another advantage to practicing *maraṇānusati* from time to time. One thinks, "Who knows for how many lives I have been rolling in this cycle of existence? This time, as a result of some wholesome deed, I have obtained the invaluable life of a human being; I have come in contact with pure Dhamma; I have developed faith in Dhamma, free from meaningless rituals, philosophies, and sectarian barriers. But what benefit have I derived from this?"

Having made this assessment, whatever shortcomings one finds, one develops enthusiasm to correct them. Whether death will come tomorrow morning or after 100 autumns, I do not know. But no matter how many days I have to live, I will use them to perfect my *pāramitās* with a contented mind and make my human life meaningful. Whatever results come, let them come; whenever they come, let them come then—I leave that to Dhamma. For my part, let me continue, to the best of my ability, to make good use of the time I have remaining in this important life.

For this purpose, let these inspiring words of the Buddha remain with us:

Uttiṭṭhe nappamajjeyya dhammaṃ sucaritaṃ care.

Arise! Live the Dhamma life with diligence.

Keep living the life of Dhamma and the results will naturally be beneficial.

—S.N. Goenka

Tumhehi kiccaṃātappaṃ,
akkhātāro tathāgatā;
paṭipannā pamokkhanti,
jhāyino mārabandhanā.

You yourself must make the effort;
the Enlightened Ones only show the way.
Those who practice meditation
will free themselves from the chains of death.

—*Dhammapada* 20.276

Sabbapāpassa akaraṇaṃ,
kusalassa upasampadā;
sacittapariyodapanaṃ,
etaṃ buddhāna sāsanaṃ.

Abstain from evil actions;
perform pious actions;
purify your mind.
This is the teaching of all the Buddhas.

—*Dhammapada* 14.183

The Buddha did not teach suffering. He taught the way leading to happiness. But you have to work with full effort and without wavering. Even though your limbs ache, do not give up. Know that wise people of the past have walked on the same path.

—Venerable Webu Sayadaw

Appendix

The Art of Living: Vipassana Meditation

based on a public talk by S.N. Goenka, delivered in Bern, Switzerland

Everyone seeks peace and harmony, because this is what we lack in our lives. From time to time we all experience agitation, irritation, disharmony. And when we suffer from these miseries, we don't keep them to ourselves; we often distribute them to others as well. Unhappiness permeates the atmosphere around someone who is miserable, and those who come in contact with such a person also become affected. Certainly this is not a skillful way to live.

We ought to live at peace with ourselves and at peace with others. After all, human beings are social beings, having to live in society and deal with each other. But how are we to live peacefully? How are we to remain harmonious within, and maintain peace and harmony around us, so that others can also live peacefully and harmoniously?

In order to be relieved of our misery, we have to know the basic reason for it, the cause of the suffering. If we investigate the problem, it becomes clear that whenever we start generating any negativity or impurity in the mind, we are bound to become unhappy. Negativity in the mind, a mental defilement or impurity, cannot coexist with peace and harmony.

How do we start generating negativity? Again, by investigating, it becomes clear. We become unhappy when we find someone behaving in a way that we don't like, or when we find something happening that we don't like. Unwanted things happen and we create tension within. Wanted things do not happen, some obstacle comes in the way, and again we create tension within—we start tying knots within. And throughout life, unwanted things keep on happening, wanted things may or may not happen, and this process of reaction, of tying knots—

Gordian knots—makes the entire mental and physical structure so tense, so full of negativity, that life becomes miserable.

Now, one way to solve this problem is to arrange that nothing unwanted happens in life—that everything keeps happening exactly as we desire. Either we must develop the power, or somebody else who will come to our aid must have the power, to see that unwanted things do not happen and that everything we want happens. But this is impossible. There is no one in the world whose desires are always fulfilled, in whose life everything happens according to his or her wishes, without anything unwanted happening. Things constantly occur that are contrary to our desires and wishes. So the question arises: how can we stop reacting blindly when confronted with things that we don't like? How can we stop creating tension and remain peaceful and harmonious?

In India, as well as in other countries, wise saintly persons of the past studied this problem—the problem of human suffering—and found a solution. If something unwanted happens and you start to react by generating anger, fear or any negativity, then, as soon as possible, you should divert your attention to something else. For example, get up, take a glass of water, start drinking—your anger won't multiply; on the other hand, it'll begin to subside. Or start counting: one, two, three, four. Or start repeating a word, or a phrase, or some mantra, perhaps the name of a god or saintly person towards whom you have devotion. The mind is diverted, and to some extent you'll be free of the negativity, free of the anger.

This solution was helpful; it worked. It still works. Responding like this, the mind feels free from agitation. However, the solution works only at the conscious level. In fact, by diverting the attention you push the negativity deep into the unconscious, and there you continue to generate and multiply the same defilement. On the surface there is a layer of peace and harmony, but in the depths of the mind there is a sleeping volcano of suppressed negativity that sooner or later may erupt in a violent explosion.

Other explorers of inner truth went still further in their search and, by experiencing the reality of mind and matter within themselves, recognized that diverting the attention is only running away from the problem. Escape is no solution; you have to face the problem. Whenever negativity arises in the mind, just observe it, face it. As soon as you start to observe a mental impurity, it begins to lose its strength and slowly withers away.

A good solution; it avoids both extremes—suppression and expression. Burying the negativity in the unconscious will not eradicate it, and allowing it to manifest as unwholesome physical or vocal actions will only create more problems. But if you just observe, then the defilement passes away and you are free of it.

This sounds wonderful, but is it really practical? It's not easy to face one's own impurities. When anger arises, it so quickly overwhelms us that we don't even notice. Then, overpowered by anger, we perform physical or vocal actions that harm ourselves and others. Later, when the anger has passed, we start crying and repenting, begging pardon from this or that person, or from God: "Oh, I made a mistake, please excuse me!" But the next time we are in a similar situation, we again react in the same way. This continual repenting doesn't help at all.

The difficulty is that we are not aware when negativity starts. It begins deep in the unconscious mind, and by the time it reaches the conscious level it has gained so much strength that it overwhelms us, and we cannot observe it.

Suppose, then, that I employ a private secretary, so that whenever anger arises he says to me, "Look, anger is starting!" Since I cannot know when this anger will start, I'll need to hire three private secretaries for three shifts, around the clock! Let's say I can afford it, and anger begins to arise. At once my secretary tells me, "Oh look—anger has started!" The first thing I'll do is rebuke him: "You fool! You think you're paid to teach me?" I'm so overpowered by anger that good advice won't help.

Perhaps wisdom does prevail and I don't scold him. Instead, I say, "Thank you very much. Now I must sit down and observe my anger." Yet, is it possible? As soon as I close my eyes and try to observe anger, the object of the anger immediately comes into my mind—the person or incident which initiated the anger. Then I'm not observing the anger itself; I'm merely observing the external stimulus of that emotion. This will only serve to multiply the anger, and is therefore no solution. It is very difficult to observe any abstract negativity, abstract emotion, divorced from the external object that originally caused it to arise.

However, someone who reached the ultimate truth found a real solution. He discovered that whenever any impurity arises in the mind, physically two things start happening simultaneously. One is that the breath loses its normal rhythm. We start breathing harder whenever negativity comes into the mind. This is easy to observe. At a subtler level, a biochemical reaction starts in the body, resulting in some sensation. Every impurity will generate some sensation or other within the body.

This presents a practical solution. An ordinary person cannot observe abstract defilements of the mind—abstract fear, anger or passion. But with proper training and practice it is very easy to observe respiration and body sensations, both of which are directly related to mental defilements.

Respiration and sensations will help in two ways. First, they will be like private secretaries. As soon as negativity arises in the mind, the breath will lose its normality; it will start shouting, "Look, something has gone wrong!" And we cannot scold the breath; we have to accept the warning. Similarly, the sensations will tell us that something has gone wrong. Then, having been warned, we can start observing the respiration, start observing the sensations, and very quickly we find that the negativity passes away.

This mental-physical phenomenon is like a coin with two sides. On one side are the thoughts and emotions arising in the mind; on the other side are the respiration and sensations in the body. Any thoughts or emotions, any mental impurities that arise manifest themselves in the breath and the sensations of that moment. Thus, by observing the respiration or the sensations, we are in fact observing mental impurities. Instead of running away from the problem, we are facing reality as it is. As a result, we discover that these impurities lose their strength; they no longer overpower us as they did in the past. If we persist, they eventually disappear altogether and we begin to live a peaceful and happy life, a life increasingly free of negativities.

In this way the technique of self-observation shows us reality in its two aspects, inner and outer. Previously we only looked outward, missing the inner truth. We always looked outside for the cause of our unhappiness; we always blamed and tried to change the reality outside. Being ignorant of the inner reality, we never understood that the cause of suffering lies within, in our own blind reactions toward pleasant and unpleasant sensations.

Now, with training, we can see the other side of the coin. We can be aware of our breathing and also of what is happening inside. Whatever it is, breath or sensation, we learn just to observe it without losing our mental balance. We stop reacting and multiplying our misery. Instead, we allow the defilements to manifest and pass away.

The more one practices this technique, the more quickly negativities will dissolve. Gradually the mind becomes free of defilements, becomes pure. A pure mind is always full of love—selfless love for all others, full of compassion for the failings and sufferings of others, full of joy at their success and happiness, full of equanimity in the face of any situation.

When one reaches this stage, the entire pattern of one's life changes. It is no longer possible to do anything vocally or physically which will disturb the peace and happiness of others. Instead, a balanced mind not only becomes peaceful, but the surrounding atmosphere also becomes permeated with peace and harmony, and this will start affecting others, helping others too.

By learning to remain balanced in the face of everything experienced inside, one develops detachment towards all that one encounters in external situations as well. However, this detachment is not escapism or indifference to the problems of the world. Those who regularly practice Vipassana become more sensitive to the sufferings of others, and do their utmost to relieve suffering in whatever way they can—not with any agitation, but with a mind full of love, compassion and equanimity. They learn holy indifference—how to be fully committed, fully involved in helping others, while at the same time maintaining balance of mind. In this way they remain peaceful and happy, while working for the peace and happiness of others.

This is what the Buddha taught: an art of living. He never established or taught any religion, any "ism." He never instructed those who came to him to practice any rites or rituals, any empty formalities. Instead, he taught them just to observe nature as it is, by observing the reality inside. Out of ignorance we keep reacting in ways that harm ourselves and others. But when wisdom arises—the wisdom of observing reality as it is—this habit of reacting falls away. When we cease to react blindly, then we are capable of real action—action proceeding from a balanced mind, a mind that sees and understands the truth. Such action can only be positive, creative, helpful to ourselves and to others.

What is necessary, then, is to "know thyself"—advice which every wise person has given. We must know ourselves, not just intellectually in the realm of ideas and theories, and not just emotionally or devotionally, simply accepting blindly what we have heard or read. Such knowledge is not enough. Rather, we must know reality experientially. We must experience directly the reality of this mental-physical phenomenon. This alone will help us be free of our suffering.

This direct experience of our own inner reality, this technique of self-observation, is what is called Vipassana meditation. In the language of India in the time of the Buddha, *passanā* meant seeing in the ordinary way, with one's eyes open; but *vipassanā* is observing things as they actually are, not just as they appear to be. Apparent truth has to be penetrated, until we reach the ultimate truth of the entire psycho-physical structure. When we experience this truth, then we learn to stop reacting blindly, to stop creating negativities—and naturally the old ones are gradually eradicated. We become liberated from misery and experience true happiness.

There are three steps to the training given in a meditation course. First, one must abstain from any action, physical or vocal, that disturbs the peace and harmony of others. One cannot work to liberate oneself from impurities of the mind while at the same time continuing to perform deeds of body and speech that only multiply them. Therefore, a code of morality is the essential first step of the practice. One undertakes not to kill, not to steal, not to commit sexual misconduct, not to tell lies, and not to use intoxicants. By abstaining from such actions, one allows the mind to quiet down sufficiently in order to proceed further.

The next step is to develop some mastery over this wild mind by training it to remain fixed on a single object, the breath. One tries to keep one's attention on the respiration for as long as possible. This is not a breathing exercise; one does not regulate the breath. Instead, one observes natural respiration as it is, as it comes in, as it goes out. In this way one further calms the mind so that it is no longer overpowered by intense negativities. At the same time, one is concentrating the mind, making it sharp and penetrating, capable of the work of insight.

These first two steps, living a moral life, and controlling the mind, are very necessary and beneficial in themselves, but they will lead to suppression of negativities unless one takes the third step: purifying the mind of defilements by developing insight into one's own nature. This is Vipassana: experiencing one's own reality by the systematic and dispassionate observation within oneself of the ever-changing mind-matter phenomenon manifesting as sensations. This is the culmination of the teaching of the Buddha: self-purification by self-observation.

It can be practiced by one and all. Everyone faces the problem of suffering. It is a universal malady that requires a universal remedy, not a sectarian one. When one suffers from anger, it's not Buddhist anger, Hindu anger, or Christian anger. Anger is anger. When one becomes agitated as a result of this anger, this agitation is not Christian, or Jewish, or Muslim. The malady is universal. The remedy must also be universal.

Vipassana is such a remedy. No one will object to a code of living which respects the peace and harmony of others. No one will object to developing control over the mind. No one will object to developing insight into one's own nature, by which it is possible to free the mind of negativities. Vipassana is a universal path.

Observing reality as it is by observing the truth inside—this is knowing oneself directly and experientially. As one practices, one keeps freeing oneself from the misery of mental impurities. From the gross, external, apparent truth, one penetrates to the ultimate truth of mind and matter. Then one transcends that, and experiences a truth that is beyond mind and matter, beyond time and space, beyond the conditioned field of relativity: the truth of total liberation from all defilements, all impurities, all suffering. Whatever name one gives this ultimate truth is irrelevant; it is the final goal of everyone.

May you all experience this ultimate truth. May all people be free from misery. May they enjoy real peace, real harmony, real happiness.

May all beings be happy.

—S.N. Goenka

The Practice of *Mettā Bhāvanā* in Vipassana Meditation

a paper presented at the Seminar on Vipassana Meditation, convened at Dhamma Giri, India, in December 1986

The practice of *mettā-bhāvanā* (meditation of loving-kindness) is an important adjunct to the technique of Vipassana meditation—indeed, its logical outcome. In *mettā-bhāvanā* one radiates loving-kindness and good will toward all beings, deliberately charging the atmosphere around with calming, positive vibrations of pure and compassionate love. Buddha instructed his followers to develop *mettā* in order to lead more peaceful and harmonious lives, and to help others do so as well. Students of Vipassana are encouraged to follow that instruction because *mettā* is the way to share with all others the peace and harmony we are developing.

The *Tipiṭaka* commentaries state: *Mijjati siniyhatiṛti mettā*—"That which inclines one to a friendly disposition is *mettā*." It is a sincere wish, without a trace of ill will, for the good and welfare of all. *Adosoṛti mettā*—"Non-aversion is *mettā*." The chief characteristic of *mettā* is a benevolent attitude. It culminates in the identification of oneself with all beings—recognition of the fellowship of all life.

To grasp this concept at least intellectually is easy enough, but it is far harder to develop this attitude in oneself. To do so some practice is needed, and so we have the technique of *mettā-bhāvanā*, the systematic cultivation of good will toward others. To be really effective, *mettā* meditation must be practiced along with Vipassana meditation. So long as negativities such as aversion dominate the mind, it is futile to formulate conscious thoughts of good will, and doing so would be merely a ritual devoid of inner meaning. However, when negativities are removed by the practice of Vipassana, good will naturally wells up in the mind. Emerging from the prison of self-obsession, we begin to concern ourselves with the welfare of others.

For this reason, the technique of *mettā-bhāvanā* is introduced only at the end of a Vipassana course, after the participants have passed through the process of purification. At such a time meditators often feel a deep wish for the well-being of others, making their practice of *mettā* truly effective. Though limited time is devoted to it in a course, *mettā* may be regarded as the culmination of the practice of Vipassana.

Nibbāna can be experienced only by those whose minds are filled with loving-kindness and compassion for all beings. Simply wishing for that state is not enough: we must purify our minds to attain it. We do so by Vipassana meditation; hence the emphasis on this technique during a course.

As we practice, we become aware that the underlying reality of the world, ourselves included, is a moment-to-moment arising and passing away. We realize that the process of change continues beyond our control and regardless of our wishes. Gradually we understand that any attachment to what is ephemeral and insubstantial produces suffering for us. We learn to be detached and to keep the balance of our minds in the face of any transient phenomena. Then we begin to experience what real happiness is: not the satisfaction of desire or the forestalling of fear, but rather liberation from the cycle of desire and fear. As inner serenity develops, we clearly see how others are enmeshed in suffering, and naturally the wish arises, "May they find what we have found: the way out of misery, the path of peace." This is the proper volition for the practice of *mettā-bhāvanā.*

Mettā is not prayer, nor is it the hope that an outside agency will help. On the contrary, it is a dynamic process producing a supportive atmosphere in which others can act to help themselves. *Mettā* can be directed toward a particular person or it may be omnidirectional. The realization that *mettā* is not produced by us makes its transmission truly selfless.

In order to conduct *mettā*, the mind must be calm, balanced, and free from negativity. This is the type of mind developed in the practice of Vipassana. A meditator knows by experience how anger, antipathy, or ill will destroy peace and frustrate any effort to help others. Only as hatred is removed and equanimity developed can we be happy and wish happiness for others. The words "May all beings be happy" have great force only when uttered from a pure mind. Backed by this purity, they will certainly be effective in fostering the happiness of others.

We must therefore examine ourselves before practicing *mettā-bhāvanā* to check whether we are really capable of transmitting *mettā*. If we find even a tinge of hatred or aversion in our minds, we should refrain at that time; otherwise, we would transmit that negativity, causing harm to others. However, if mind and body are filled with serenity and well-being, it is natural and appropriate to share this happiness with others: "May you be happy; may you be liberated from the defilements that are the causes of suffering. May all beings be peaceful."

This loving attitude enables us to deal far more skillfully with the vicissitudes of life. Suppose, for example, one encounters a person who is acting out of deliberate ill will to harm others. The common response—to react with fear and hatred—is self-centered, does nothing to improve the situation and, in fact, magnifies the negativity. It would be far more helpful to remain calm and balanced, with a feeling of good will, especially for the person who is acting wrongly. This must not be merely an intellectual stance, a veneer over unresolved negativity. *Mettā* works only when it is the spontaneous outflow of a purified mind.

The serenity gained in Vipassana meditation naturally gives rise to feelings of *mettā*, and throughout the day this will continue to affect us and our environment in a positive way. Thus, Vipassana ultimately has a dual function: to bring us happiness by purifying our minds, and to help us foster the happiness of others by preparing us to practice *mettā*. What, after all, is the purpose of freeing ourselves of negativity and egotism unless we share these benefits with others? In a retreat we temporarily cut ourselves off from the world in order to return and share with others what we have gained in solitude. These two aspects of the practice of Vipassana are inseparable.

In these times of widespread malaise, economic disparity, and violent unrest, the need for *mettā-bhāvanā* is greater than ever. If peace and harmony are to reign throughout the world, they must first be established in the minds of all its inhabitants.

Acknowledgments

Most of the articles contained in this anthology bear the name of Mr. S.N. Goenka (SNG). The editors would like to express their gratitude to Goenkaji and the Vipassana Research Institute (VRI), Igatpuri, India, for use of this material.

Articles from the *Vipassana Newsletter* include: "My Mother's Death in Dhamma" by SNG, "As It Was / As It Is" by Graham Gambie, "Tara Jadhav: An Exemplary Death" by SNG, "Kamma—The Real Inheritance" by SNG, "Ratilal Mehta: A Life and Death in Dhamma" by SNG, "Parvathamma Adaviappa: Equanimity in the Face of Terminal Illness" by Mr. S. Adaviappa, "Work Out Your Own Salvation" by SNG, and "Seventy Years Are Over" by SNG.

Other material from VRI includes: "What Vipassana Is", "The Art of Living: Vipassana Meditation", "The Practice of Mettā Bhāvanā in Vipassana Meditation" and the *Glossary*, as well as different quotation and scriptural translations by SNG and Sayagyi U Ba Khin. All Hindi *dohas* (couplets) are from *Come People of the World* by SNG. *Questions To Goenkaji, Parts I, II, and III* came from various sources, including the *Vipassana Newsletter* and private interviews.

"Graham's Death" by Anne Doneman previously appeared in *Realizing Change* by Ian Hetherington, Vipassana Research Publications.

"What Happens at Death" by SNG first appeared in the *Sayagyi U Ba Khin Journal*, VRI.

"Paṭicca Samuppāda—The Law of Dependent Origination" is from *The Discourse Summaries*, Day 5, VRI.

Quotations from the Venerable Webu Sayadaw are from *The Way to Ultimate Calm*, translated by Roger Bischoff, Buddhist Publication Society 2001.

Material for *Living in the Present Moment* and *Facing Death Head-on* originated in private interviews with Susan Babbitt, and with Terrell and Diane Jones. Part of *Living in the Present*

Moment was also published as *Join the Cosmic Dance*, Thee Hellbox Press.

The Rodney Bernier interview, *Smiling All the Way to Death,* was provided by Evie Chauncey.

The Flood of Tears translated by C.A.F. Rhys Davids was taken from *The Book of Kindred Sayings Part II*, Pali Text Society.

The *Undying Gratitude* letter by John Wolford was supplied by John's mother, Laurie Campbell. Thanks also to Laurie and to Gabriela Ionita for granting permission to print their personal letters to Goenkaji.

Ambapāḷī's Verses—translated by Amadeo Solé-Leris, from *Great Disciples of the Buddha: Their Lives, Their Works, Their Legacy,* by Nyanaponika Thera and Helmuth Hecker. Copyright 2003 by Buddhist Publication Society. Reprinted with the permission of The Permissions Company, Inc., on behalf of Wisdom Publications, www.wisdompubs.org.

Dhammapada verses 41, 128, 165, 288 and 289 are Harischandra Kaviratna's translation, courtesy of the Theosophical University Press, Pasadena, California.

Paṭhama-ākāsa Sutta appeared in the *Vipassana Journal*, VRI.

Aṅguttara Nikāya II, 10, Translated by Ven. S. Dhammika, is in *Gemstones of the Good Dhamma*, Buddhist Publication Society.

The sources of other *Tipiṭaka* verses quoted are, unfortunately, unknown. The editors sincerely apologize to the rightful translators for using their work without citations.

Front cover designed by Irek Sroka, and back cover designed by Julie Schaeffer.

Photo credits: Graham Gambie courtesy of Anne Donemon, Rodney Bernier taken by Patrick McKay, and Ratilal Metha courtesy of Himanshu Mehta.

Line editing done by Luke Matthews, Ben Baroncini, Michael Solomon, Peter Greene, William Hart, Frank Tedesco, Julie Schaeffer, and others.

Photo editing done by Eric M. Madigan.

Finally, thanks to my husband Bill for his wisdom and unfailing patience while assisting with the preparation of this anthology in all its stages.

Glossary

Included in this list are Pāḷi (and some Hindi and Burmese) terms that appear in the text.

ānāpāna – Respiration; inhalation-exhalation. Frequently used as a shortened version of *ānāpāna-sati*: Awareness of respiration.

anattā – Not self, egoless, without essence, without substance. One of the three basic characteristics of phenomena, along with *anicca* and *dukkha.*

anicca – Impermanent, ephemeral, changing. One of the three basic characteristics of phenomena, along with *anattā* and *dukkha.*

arahant – Liberated being; one who has completely destroyed all mental impurities.

bhāva – Becoming; the continuity of life and death.

bhāvanā – Mental development; meditation. The two divisions of *bhāvanā* are the development of tranquility (*samatha-bhāvanā*), concentration of mind (*samādhi*); and the development of insight (*vipassanā-bhāvanā*), wisdom (*paññā*). Development of *samatha* leads to states of mental absorption; development of *vipassanā* leads to liberation.

bhāvatu sabba maṅgalaṃ – Traditional wish of good will—literally, "May all beings be well, be happy."

bhikkhu – Monk; meditator.

bhikkhunī – Nun; meditator.

brahma-loka – One of the 20 highest planes of existence.

Buddha – Enlightened person; one who discovers the way to liberation, practices it, and reaches the final goal by his own efforts.

dāna – Generosity, charity; donation.

deva – Deity; a heavenly being. Also, *devaputta* – son of a *deva*.

dhamma – Phenomenon; object of mind; nature; natural law; law of liberation, i.e., teaching of an enlightened person. (Sanskrit, *dharma*.)

doha – (Hindi) Rhyming couplet.

dukkha – Suffering, unsatisfactoriness; one of the three basic characteristics of phenomena, along with *anattā* and *anicca*.

gāthā – Verse of poetry.

Gotama – Clan or family name of the historical Buddha. (Sanskrit, *Gautama*)

Goenkaji – Mr. S.N. Goenka. The suffix "-ji" indicates affection and respect.

Jainism – Ancient, non-theistic, Indian religion stressing nonviolence, morality, wisdom, and the necessity of self-effort to achieve liberation.

kāma – Desire, sensual pleasure.

kamma – Action; specifically, a mental, verbal, or physical action producing an effect. (Sanskrit, *karma*.)

loka – Universe; world; plane of existence.

maṅgala – Welfare, blessing, happiness.

maraṇānusati – Awareness of death.

Mataji – (Hindi) Mother. In this context, Mrs. Goenka.

mettā – Loving-kindness; selfless love, good will.

mettā bhāvanā – systematic cultivation of *mettā* through meditation.

nibbāna – Extinction; freedom from suffering, liberation; the ultimate reality; the unconditioned. (Sanskrit, *nirvāṇa*)

Pāli – Line; text. Texts recording the teaching of the Buddha, hence the language of these texts. Historical, linguistic, and archaeological evidence indicates that *Pāli* was spoken in northern India at or near the time of the Buddha.

paññā – Wisdom. Third of the three trainings by which the Noble Eightfold Path is practiced. See *ariya aṭṭhaṅgika magga*. There are three kinds of wisdom: *suta-mayā paññā* (received wisdom, i.e., wisdom gained from listening to others); *cintā-mayā paññā* (wisdom gained by intellectual analysis); and *bhāvanā-mayā paññā* (wisdom developed by direct, personal experience). Only *bhāvanā-mayā paññā*, cultivated by the practice of *vipassanā-bhāvanā*, can totally purify the mind.

pāramī / pāramitā – Perfection, virtue; wholesome mental qualities.

paṭicca-samuppāda – Dependent origination, conditioned arising, causal genesis. The process, born of ignorance, by which beings generate suffering.

rūpa – Matter; visual object.

sādhu – "Well done; well said." Traditional expression of approval or agreement, usually spoken three times.

samādhi – Concentration, control of one's mind. Second of the three trainings by which the Noble Eightfold Path is practiced. See *ariya aṭṭhaṅgika magga*. When cultivated as an end in itself, leads to the attainment of the states of mental absorption (*jhāna*), but not to total liberation of mind.

saṃsāra – Cycle of rebirth; conditioned world; realm of suffering.

saṅkhāra – Volitional activity; mental formation or mental conditioning; mental reaction. One of the four mental aggregates or processes, along with *viññāṇa*, *saññā*, and *vedanā*. (Sanskrit, *samskāra*.)

saññā – Perception, recognition. One of the four mental aggregates or processes, along with *viññāṇa, vedanā*, and *saṅkhāra*. *Saññā* is conditioned by one's past *saṅkhāras* and therefore conveys a distorted image of reality. In the practice of Vipassana, *saññā* changes to *paññā*, the understanding of reality as it is: *anicca-saññā, dukkha-saññā, anattā-saññā, asubhasaññā*—perception of impermanence, of suffering, of no-self, of the illusory nature of beauty.

sāsana – Dispensation of a Buddha; period of time in which the teaching of a Buddha is available.

sati – Awareness. *Ānāpāna-sati* – awareness of respiration. *Sammā-sati* – right awareness, a constituent of the Noble Eightfold Path. See *ariya aṭṭhaṅgika magga*.

satipaṭṭhāna – Establishing of awareness, in four aspects:

kāyānupassanā – of the body,

vedanānupassanā – of sensations within the body,

cittānupassanā – of mind,

dhammānupassanā – of mental contents.

All four are included in the observation of *vedanā* since sensations are directly related to both body and mind.

sayadaw – (Burmese) Literally, "royal teacher." Abbot or senior monk of a monastery.

sayagyi – (Burmese) Lit. "big teacher." An honorific or respectful title.

sīla – Morality, abstention from physical and vocal actions that harm oneself or others. First of the three trainings by which the Noble Eightfold Path is practiced. See *ariya aṭṭhaṅgika magga*.

sutta – Discourse attributed to the Buddha or one of his leading disciples. (Sanskrit, *sutra.*)

Tipiṭaka – Literally, "three baskets." (Sanskrit, *tripiṭaka*)

The three collections of the teachings of the Buddha:

vinaya-piṭaka – monastic discipline,

sutta-piṭaka – discourses,

abhidhamma-piṭaka – systematic philosophical exegesis of the Dhamma.

U – (Burmese) Mister.

vedanā – Sensation; bodily feeling. One of the four mental aggregates or processes, along with *viññāṇa*, *saññā*, and *saṅkhāra*. According to the doctrine of Dependent Origination, *taṇhā* (craving), arises dependent on *vedanā* (sensation). See *paṭicca-samuppāda***.** Having both mental and physical aspects, *vedanā* is a convenient object for investigation of body and mind. By learning to observe *vedanā* objectively, one can avoid new reactions of craving or aversion, and experience directly within oneself the reality of *anicca* (impermanence). This experience is essential for the development of *upekkhā* (equanimity), leading to liberation of the mind.

viññāṇa – Consciousness, cognition. One of the four mental aggregates or processes, along with *saññā*, *vedanā*, and *saṅkhāra*.

vipassanā – Literally, "seeing in a special way." Introspection. Insight that purifies the mind; specifically, insight into the impermanent, unsatisfactory, and substanceless nature of mind and body. Also, *vipassanā-bhāvanā* – the systematic development of insight through observation of sensations within the body.

Pragyā jāge balavatī,
aṅga-aṅga rama jāya.
Aṇu-aṇu cetana ho uṭhe,
cita nirmala ho jāya.

May wisdom arise, mighty in power,
and spread throughout your being,
enlivening every atom
and purifying the mind.

—Hindi *doha,* S.N. Goenka

About Pariyatti

Pariyatti is dedicated to providing affordable access to authentic teachings of the Buddha about the Dhamma theory (*pariyatti*) and practice (*paṭipatti*) of Vipassana meditation. A 501(c)(3) non- profit charitable organization since 2002, Pariyatti is sustained by contributions from individuals who appreciate and want to share the incalculable value of the Dhamma teachings. We invite you to visit www.pariyatti.org to learn about our programs, services, and ways to support publishing and other undertakings.

Pariyatti Publishing Imprints

Vipassana Research Publications (focus on Vipassana as taught by S.N. Goenka in the tradition of Sayagyi U Ba Khin)

BPS Pariyatti Editions (selected titles from the Buddhist Publica- tion Society, copublished by Pariyatti in the Americas)

Pariyatti Digital Editions (audio and video titles, including dis- courses)

Pariyatti Press (classic titles returned to print and inspirational writing by contemporary authors)

Pariyatti enriches the world by

- disseminating the words of the Buddha,
- providing sustenance for the seeker's journey,
- illuminating the meditator's path.

Courses of Vipassana meditation as taught by S.N. Goenka in the tradition of Sayagyi U Ba Khin are held regularly in many countries around the world.

Information, worldwide schedules and application forms are available from the Vipassana website:

www.dhamma.org